Fundamentals Pape

Corporate and Busi

First edition 2007, Ninth edition April 2015

ISBN 9781 4727 2699 5

e ISBN 9781 4727 2764 0

British Library Cataloguing-in-Publication Data

A catalogue record for this book is available from the British Library

Published by

BPP Learning Media Ltd
BPP House, Aldine Place
142–144 Uxbridge Road
London W12 8AA

www.bpp.com/learningmedia

Printed in the UK by

Ashford Colour Press Ltd
Unit 600 Fareham Reach
Fareham Road, Gosport
Hampshire PO13 0FW

Your learning materials, published by BPP Learning Media Ltd, are printed on paper obtained from traceable sustainable sources.

Welcome to BPP Learning Media's new syllabus ACCA **Passcards for Fundamentals Paper F4 Corporate and Business Law (Eng)**.

- They **focus on your exam** and **save you time**.

- They incorporate **diagrams** to kick start your memory.

- They follow the overall **structure** of the BPP Learning Media Study Texts, but BPP Learning Media's ACCA **Passcards** are not just a condensed book. Each card has been separately designed for clear presentation. Topics are self contained and can be grasped visually.

- ACCA **Passcards** are still **just the right size** for pockets, briefcases and bags.

Run through the **Passcards** as often as you can during your final revision period. The day before the exam, try to go through the **Passcards** again! You will then be well on your way to passing your exams.

Good luck!

Contents

1: Law and the legal system

Topic List

This chapter explains some basic principles of English law and how the system of courts operates.

What is law?

'**Law is a formal mechanism of social control**',
Business Law 5th Edition, David Kelly, Ann Holmes and Ruth Hayward

Types of law

Common law and equity

The **earliest elements** of the English legal system.

Common law is judge-made law which developed by amalgamating local customary laws into one 'law of the land'. Remedies are monetary.

Equity was brought in to introduce fairness into the legal system and offers alternative remedies when money is not sufficient.

Statute law

This is law **created by Parliament** in the form of statutes.

Statute law is usually made in areas so complicated or unique that common law alternatives are unlikely or would take too long to develop.

Private law and public law

Private law deals with relationships between private individuals, groups or organisations.

The state provides the legal framework (such as statutes) that allows individuals to handle the matters themselves. The state does not get involved.

Public law is concerned with government and the functions of public organisations.

The key difference between public and private law is that it is the **state** that **prosecutes** under **public law** whereas the individual takes up the action in private law.

Criminal law and criminal liability

A **crime** is conduct prohibited by law. Crimes are punishable, usually by fine or imprisonment.

The state prosecutes. It must prove **beyond reasonable doubt** that the accused committed the crime.

Civil law and civil liability

Civil law exists to regulate disputes over the rights and obligations of persons dealing with each other.

The claimant must prove on **balance of probabilities** that the defendant caused the damage. A key area for businesses is **contract**.

The distinction is not the act but the legal consequences.

Civil

The simplified diagram below sets out the English civil court structure.

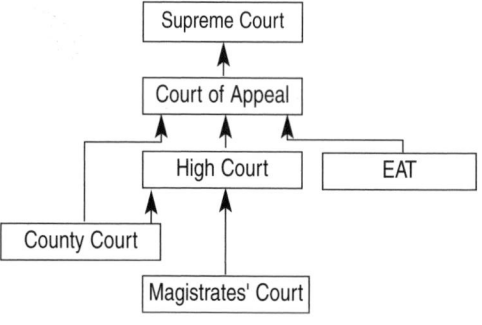

Criminal

The simplified diagram below sets out the English criminal court structure.

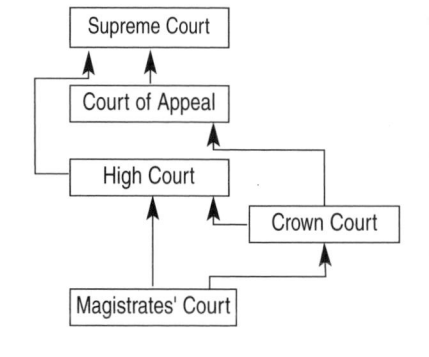

Note. EAT means the Employment Appeals Tribunal.

Status of courts

Function	Appeals to	Bound by	Binds
Magistrates' Court			
Tries minor crimes summarily Committals to Crown Court Limited family and other civil jurisdiction	Crown Court High Court	High Court Court of Appeal Supreme Court ECJ	No one Not even itself
County Court			
Majority of civil cases in UK Cases are allocated to one of three tracks ■ Small claims — <£10K ■ Fast track - £10K - £25K (30 wks) ■ Multi track — >£25K - High Court.	High Court Court of Appeal (civil) for multi-track cases	High Court Court of Appeal Supreme Court ECJ	No one Not even itself
Crown Court			
All indictable crimes with a jury Appeals and committals from Magistrates' Court Limited civil cases	Court of Appeal (criminal) High Court (QBD)	High Court (QBD) Court of Appeal Supreme Court ECJ	No one (However, cases are persuasive)

Function	Appeals to	Bound by	Binds
High Court			
QBD: Civil matters such as contract and tort	Court of Appeal (civil)	The relevant divisional court	Magistrates' Court
Chancery: Traditional equity matters (eg partnership, mortgages, wills)	Supreme Court (leapfrog procedure)	Court of Appeal	County Court
Family: Matrimonial, children		Supreme Court, ECJ	Crown Court
Court of Appeal			
Civil division	Supreme Court	Own decisions	All inferior UK courts
Criminal division		Supreme Court (subject to an exception); ECJ	Itself (subject to an exception)
Supreme Court			
The highest UK appeal court	ECJ	Itself (except in exceptional cases) ECJ	All UK courts Itself (usually)
ECJ			
Interpretation of EU treaties	No appeal	No one Not even itself	All UK courts

2: Sources of English law

Topic List

Case law and precedent

Legislation and statutory interpretation

Delegated legislation

Human rights

In this chapter, the sources of English law are identified and outlined.

Case law

The basis of case law is that the law is interpreted by the courts and evolves as cases are heard.

The doctrine of judicial precedent

Judicial precedent is based on the view that a function of the judge is to decide cases in accordance with existing case law. It provides consistency. A judge must follow precedents in accordance with certain rules.

Rules

- A precedent must be based on a **proposition of law**, not a decision on a question of fact.

- It must form part of the **ratio decidendi** of the case, that is, the judge's reason for deciding.

- The **material facts** of each case must be the same.

- The **status** of the previous court must be such that it binds the court seeking precedent.

- A judge may make statements 'by the way', ie, not part of the ratio. These are **obiter dicta**.

Avoidance of a binding precedent

The courts may decline to follow an apparently binding precedent by

- Distinguishing the facts
- Declaring the ratio decidendi obscure
- Stating the previous decision was made per incuriam (carelessly)
- Stating it is in conflict with a fundamental principle
- Declaring an earlier precedent too wide

Advantages and disadvantages of judicial precedent

Advantages	Disadvantages
☑ Encourages certainty and consistency ☑ Flexibility ☑ Detail ☑ Practicality	☒ Risk of illogical decisions or inconsistencies to avoid unfair result ☒ Restricts discretion of judges ☒ Bulk of case law ☒ May create unfair precedents

Extrinsic Aids - Reports, i.e. Law/Royal Commissions, Law Reform
committee
- Hansard
official journal
of parliament
debates

Legislation

Legislation or statute, is **law made by Parliament**. Parliament can make the law as it sees fit, or as directed by the EU. Parliament makes new law and repeals and overrules old law. This is known as Parliamentary sovereignty.

Statutory interpretation

Intrinsic Aids
- Side notes
- title of Act

The key rules of statutory interpretation are:

Literal rule:	plain, ordinary or literal meaning.
Purposive approach:	reference made to context and purpose of legislation. What is it trying to achieve?
Contextual rule:	looks at the statute as a whole to discover the meaning of a word.

Advantages
☑ Responsive to public opinion
☑ Can deal with any problem
☑ Carefully constructed
☑ Can respond to problems in society or case law

Disadvantages
☒ Bulky
☒ Time pressure may mean legislation lacks detail
☒ Takes up a lot of parliamentary time
☒ Cannot anticipate every possible scenario

Delegated legislation

Delegated legislation is law, often of a detailed nature, made by subordinate bodies who have been given the power to do so by statute.

Types of delegated legislation

Statutory Instruments, Bye-laws, Rules of court, Professional regulations, Orders in Council

Control of delegated legislation

- Some require positive Parliamentary approval
- Most is laid before Parliament for 40 days before enactment to allow negative resolutions
- There are Scrutiny Committees in both houses
- May be challenged in court as *ultra vires*

Acts of Parliament may contain sections giving power to ministers or public bodies to make delegated legislation for specific purposes.

Advantages

- ✓ Saves parliamentary time
- ✓ Allows technical expertise
- ✓ Allows swift alteration without referring back to Parliament

Disadvantages

- ✗ Lack of accountability
- ✗ Power given to civil servants
- ✗ Volume and complexity

The Human Rights Act 1998

The **Human Rights Act 1998** incorporates the articles of the European Convention for the Protection of Human Rights and Fundamental Freedoms into UK law. This is a convention which the UK signed in 1951, but which previously had not been given legal status in the UK. The Human Rights Act became effective in the UK in October 2000.

It continues to have far-reaching effects on UK law. Human rights cases can be brought in UK courts, with the highest court of appeal being the European Court of Human Rights. The effect of the Human Rights Act will continue to be felt over time as cases are brought to the courts.

The impact of the Human Rights Act 1998

Existing legislation

- To be interpreted in line with the Convention
- ECHR decisions to be taken into account
- Law can be declared incompatible
- Domestic law must then be amended
- Domestic law is still valid in the interim

Ministers introducing **new legislation** must:

- Make a statement of compatibility, or
- State that the government wishes to proceed anyway

Courts must take the case law of the European Court of Justice into account when making judgements.

This affects the doctrine of precedent as it permits the overruling of English law where it conflicts with the ECHR.

mischief rule : judge considers what
mischief the Act was trying to prevent.

Golden rule : words should be given
their plain ordinary or literal meaning
unless it gives + to manifest absurdity or
inconsistency with the rest of statute.

3: Formation of contract I

Topic List

This chapter provides an introduction to the law of contract. It is important to appreciate that not all contracts need to be formal written documents.

A contract

Contracts are **agreements** which **legally bind the parties**. The underlying theory is that a contract is the outcome of '**consenting minds**'.

Parties are judged by what they have **said, written or done**.

Battle of the forms

Disputes sometimes arise in commercial agreements because each party is accustomed to doing business on its own **standard terms** and argues that they apply to the contract, rather than the other party's terms.

Factors affecting the modern contract

The standard form contract

Standard form contracts are a result of mass production and consumerism. Large organisations, like electricity companies, are unlikely to negotiate individual terms with consumers.

Inequality of bargaining power

Often parties to a contract have different bargaining power. The law will intervene where experts take advantage of ordinary consumers. There should be freedom of contract.

Consumer protection

Consumer interests are served in two main areas:

- Consumer protection agencies ──■ Financial Conduct Authority
- Legislation ────────────■ *Unfair Contract Terms Act 1977*
  Consumer Credit Act 1974

Three essential contract elements

- Agreement by offer and acceptance
- Obligations of one party matched by consideration of the other
- Intention to create legal relations

Other factors affecting the validity of a contract

Capacity. Some people have restricted capacity to enter into contracts

Form. Some contracts must follow a particular form

Content. There may be some implied terms in a contract. Some express terms (such as exclusion clauses) may be unlawful

Genuine consent. There may be undue influence or duress, or misrepresentation or mistake

Legality. The courts will not enforce a contract which is illegal or contrary to public policy

Effect of failure to satisfy the validity tests

Void contract. This is no contract

Voidable contract. This contract can be avoided by one party

Unenforcable contract. This contract is valid but performance by one party cannot be forced

Form

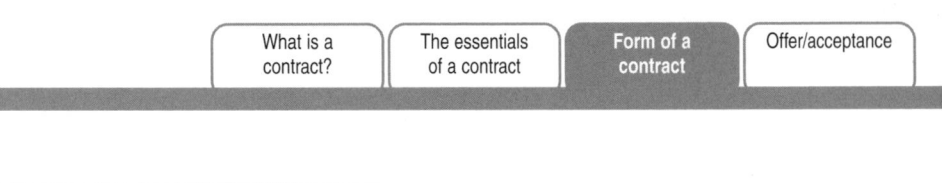

General rule: A contract can be made in any form

- Inferred
- Written   except ...
- Oral

1 Contracts by **deed**

- Leases > three years
- Conveyance for the transfer of land
- Promises not supported by consideration

2 Contracts which must be in **writing**

- Transfer of shares
- Sale of an interest in land
- Bills of exchange and cheques
- Consumer credit contracts

3 Contracts which must be **evidenced in writing**

- Contracts of guarantee

Offer

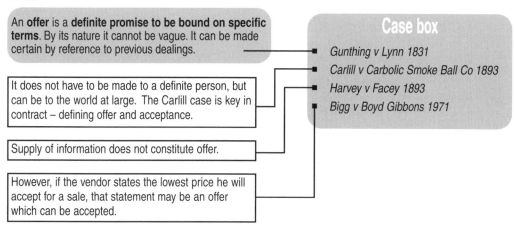

An **offer** is a **definite promise to be bound on specific terms**. By its nature it cannot be vague. It can be made certain by reference to previous dealings.

Case box

- *Gunthing v Lynn 1831*
- *Carlill v Carbolic Smoke Ball Co 1893*
- *Harvey v Facey 1893*
- *Bigg v Boyd Gibbons 1971*

It does not have to be made to a definite person, but can be to the world at large. The Carlill case is key in contract – defining offer and acceptance.

Supply of information does not constitute offer.

However, if the vendor states the lowest price he will accept for a sale, that statement may be an offer which can be accepted.

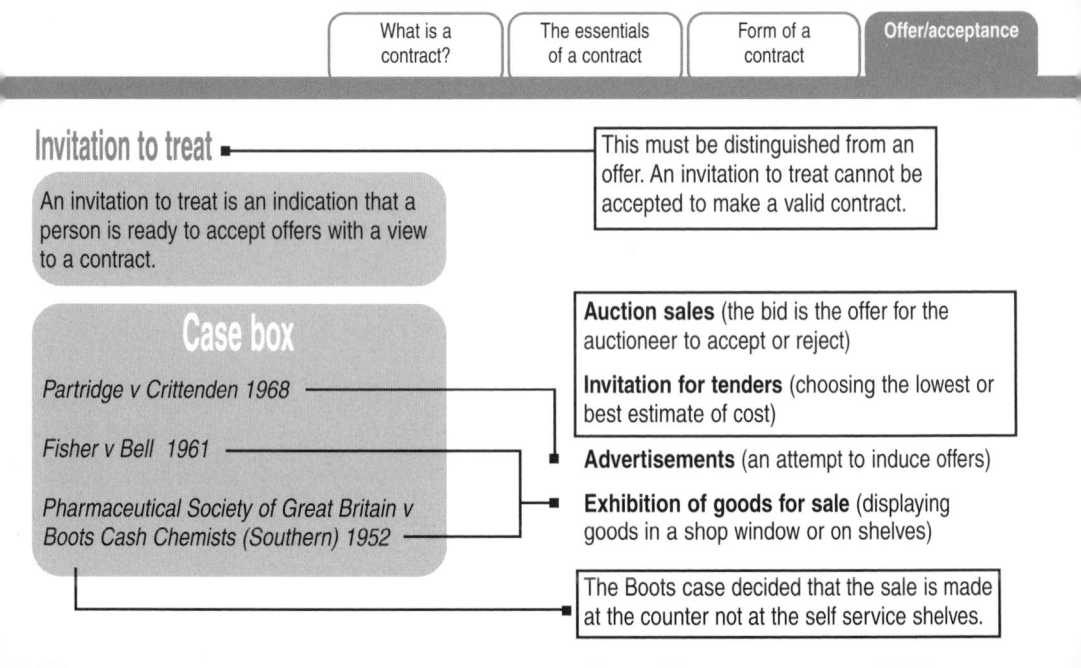

Invitation to treat

This must be distinguished from an offer. An invitation to treat cannot be accepted to make a valid contract.

An invitation to treat is an indication that a person is ready to accept offers with a view to a contract.

Case box

Partridge v Crittenden 1968

Fisher v Bell 1961

Pharmaceutical Society of Great Britain v Boots Cash Chemists (Southern) 1952

Auction sales (the bid is the offer for the auctioneer to accept or reject)

Invitation for tenders (choosing the lowest or best estimate of cost)

Advertisements (an attempt to induce offers)

Exhibition of goods for sale (displaying goods in a shop window or on shelves)

The Boots case decided that the sale is made at the counter not at the self service shelves.

Acceptance

Acceptance is a positive act by a person to whom an offer has been made. If unconditional, the act creates a binding contract.

Communication of acceptance

Acceptance must be communicated to the offeror or it is not effective.

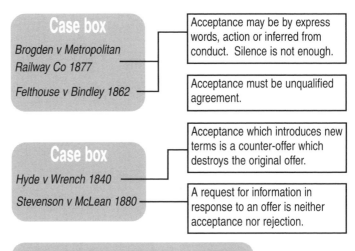

Case box

Brogden v Metropolitan Railway Co 1877

Felthouse v Bindley 1862

Acceptance may be by express words, action or inferred from conduct. Silence is not enough.

Acceptance must be unqualified agreement.

Case box

Hyde v Wrench 1840

Stevenson v McLean 1880

Acceptance which introduces new terms is a counter-offer which destroys the original offer.

A request for information in response to an offer is neither acceptance nor rejection.

Acceptance '**subject to contract**' does not bind

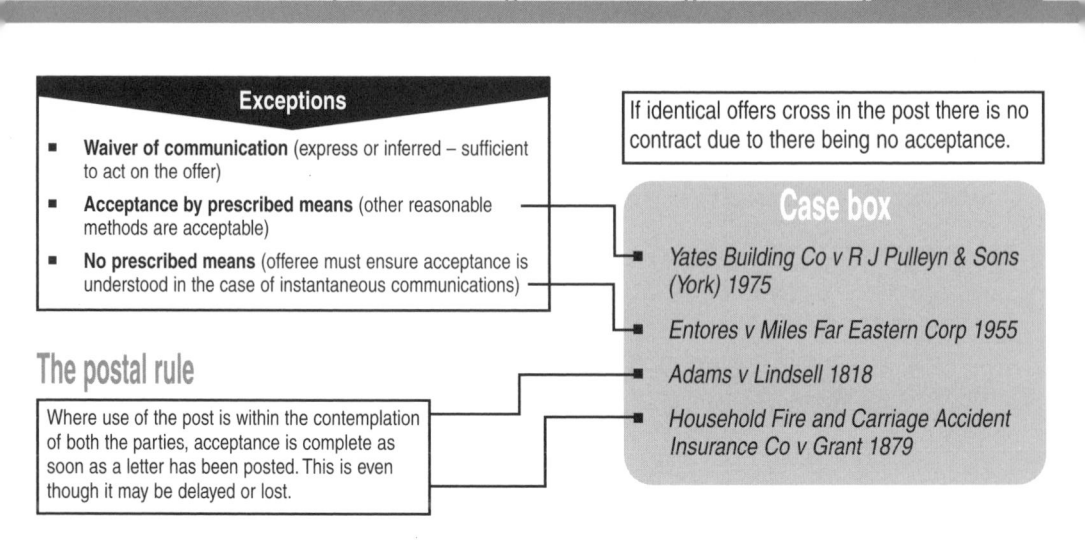

Exceptions

- **Waiver of communication** (express or inferred – sufficient to act on the offer)
- **Acceptance by prescribed means** (other reasonable methods are acceptable)
- **No prescribed means** (offeree must ensure acceptance is understood in the case of instantaneous communications)

If identical offers cross in the post there is no contract due to there being no acceptance.

Case box

- *Yates Building Co v R J Pulleyn & Sons (York) 1975*
- *Entores v Miles Far Eastern Corp 1955*
- *Adams v Lindsell 1818*
- *Household Fire and Carriage Accident Insurance Co v Grant 1879*

The postal rule

Where use of the post is within the contemplation of both the parties, acceptance is complete as soon as a letter has been posted. This is even though it may be delayed or lost.

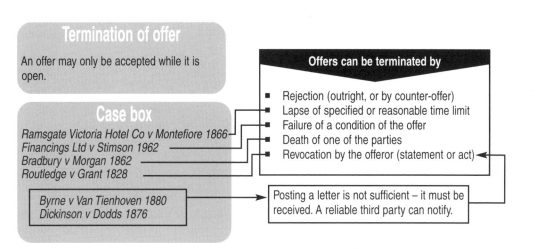

Termination of offer

An offer may only be accepted while it is open.

Case box

Ramsgate Victoria Hotel Co v Montefiore 1866
Financings Ltd v Stimson 1962
Bradbury v Morgan 1862
Routledge v Grant 1828

Byrne v Van Tienhoven 1880
Dickinson v Dodds 1876

Offers can be terminated by

- Rejection (outright, or by counter-offer)
- Lapse of specified or reasonable time limit
- Failure of a condition of the offer
- Death of one of the parties
- Revocation by the offeror (statement or act)

Posting a letter is not sufficient – it must be received. A reliable third party can notify.

Notes

4: Formation of contract II

Topic List

Consideration

Intention to create legal relations

Privity of contract

This chapter outlines the more detailed rules about the two remaining essentials of a contract:

- *Consideration*
- *Intention*

It also explains the principle of privity of contract.

Consideration

Consideration is 'some right, interest, profit or benefit accruing to one party, or some forbearance, detriment, loss or responsibility given, suffered or undertaken by the other.'

Currie v Misa 1875

Case box

Re McArdle 1951
Roscorla v Thomas 1842
Lampleigh v Braithwaite 1615
Re Casey's Patents 1892

Valid consideration

Executed consideration. This takes place at the time, eg payment for goods, on delivery.

Executory consideration. This is a promise for an act in the future, ie a promise to pay for goods later.

Past consideration

This is not valid consideration. Past consideration is anything done before a promise is made.

Exceptions
■ Bills of exchange
■ Statute barring of liability
■ Requests for services which imply liability

Adequacy and sufficiency of consideration

Consideration need not be **adequate** but must be **sufficient**.

The courts do not seek to weigh up the comparative value of promises and acts.

Consideration is considered **sufficient** if it has some **identifiable value**.

Performing existing statutory obligations is **no consideration** for promise of a reward.

However, providing **extra service is sufficient**.

There is no consideration to make extra promises binding but **further duties done creates consideration**. Rethought in modern cases, where both parties derive benefit.

Waiver of rights is **only** a **binding** promise **if** there is **consideration**.

Case box

- *Thomas v Thomas 1842*
- *Chappell & Co v Nestle Co 1960*
- *Collins v Godefroy 1831*
- *Glasbrook Bros v Glamorgan CC 1925*
- *Harris v Sheffield United FC Ltd 1988*
- *Stilk v Myrick 1809*
- *Hartley v Ponsonby 1857*
- *Williams v Roffey Bros & Nicholls (Contractors) Ltd 1990*
- *Foakes v Beer 1884*

Consideration	Intention to create legal relations	Privity of contract

Promissory estoppel

Where one party makes a promise (which is not supported by consideration), they are prevented from denying that they made the promise if it was made with the intention that the other party would rely on it.

Example of where promissory estoppel does not apply

Promissory estoppel is often argued to apply in cases where part of a debt has been written off. However, where a party writes off part of a debt just because they need the money quickly, that promise is unenforceable by the other party. The promise was not given with the intention that it would be relied upon, it was not given voluntarily.

Example of where promissory estoppel does apply

In the *High Trees* case (below) a landlord agreed to accept reduced rent because of wartime conditions. After the war they sought to recover the rent in full. However the promise was freely given and the defendants had relied on it. Therefore the reduced rent for the wartime period was upheld – special circumstances (ie the war) applied.

■ The promise of a waiver must be entirely voluntary.

Case box

Central London Property Trust v High Trees House 1947

D and C Builders v Rees 1966 ■

The principle of promissory estoppel is '**a shield not a sword**'.

Where there is no express statement as to intention to create legal relations, the courts apply **two rebuttable presumptions**:

1 Social, domestic and family arrangements are not usually intended to be binding

2 Commercial agreements are usually intended to be binding

Commercial agreements are presumed to be binding unless:

- Circumstances suggest otherwise
- It is expressly denied

> **The burden of proof is on the party seeking to escape liability.**

Relatives can intend legal relations and the courts are ready to imply them, particularly with reference to land matters.

Case box

Balfour v Balfour 1919
Merritt v Merritt 1970
Simpkins v Pays 1955
Rose and Frank v Crompton 1923
Edwards v Skyways Ltd 1964
Kleinwort Benson Ltd v Malaysia Mining Corpn Bhd 1989
Jones v Vernons Pools 1938

In contract negotiations, use of the words '**subject to contract**' amounts to a strong presumption that **no** immediately binding contract is intended.

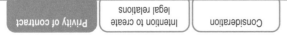

| Privity of contract | Intention to create legal relations | Consideration |

Privity of contract

Only a person who is a party to a contract has enforceable rights or obligations in it. Third parties only have a right of action in exceptional circumstances.

A maxim in contract law states 'consideration **must move from the promisee**'. Because consideration is the price of the promise, he who seeks to enforce the promise must pay.

Exceptions to the rule

- Third party can sue in another capacity
- Collateral contracts
- Valid assignment
- Foreseeable loss to third party
- Implied trusts
- Statutory exceptions
- Agency
- Restrictive covenants

Case box

- *Tweddle v Atkinson* 1861
- *Dunlop v Selfridge* 1915
- *Beswick v Beswick* 1968
- *Shanklin Pier Ltd v Detel Products Ltd* 1951
- *Linden Gardens Trust Ltd v Lenesta Sludge Disposals Ltd* 1994
- *Gregory and Parker v Williams* 1817
- *Tulk v Moxhay* 1848

5: Content of contracts

Topic List

Terms and representations

Conditions, warranties and implied terms

Exclusion clauses

Unfair terms regulations

*This is another important area in the law of contract. The distinction between **conditions** and **warranties** is a key area to grasp. Both are examples of **terms** of a contract, but they have significantly different effects if the contract is breached.*

Representations

Representations are anything which induces the contract, but do not become a **term** of the contract.

A legally binding agreement (contract) must be complete in its terms.

Exceptions

Term to be **settled by other means** (for example, market price on the day)

Courts will look at the **intention** of the **parties**

Case box

Routledge v McKay 1954

Bannerman v White 1861

Scammell v Ouston 1941

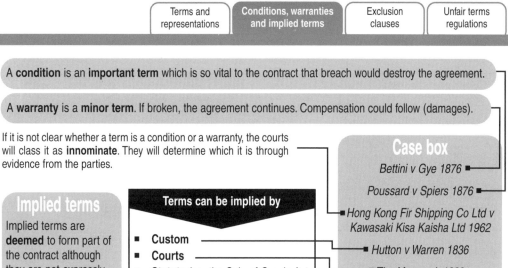

Exclusion clauses

Exclusion clauses are clauses which purport to exclude liability altogether, or to restrict it by limiting damages or by imposing other onerous conditions.

In the past they have been used in **standard form contracts** between large companies and consumers, a practice which has been strongly criticised. **Protection** is offered to consumers in two ways: **statute** (below) and **the courts** (considered here).

Protection offered to consumers by the courts ➤ The clause must be properly **incorporated** into the contract and the clauses are **interpreted** strictly.

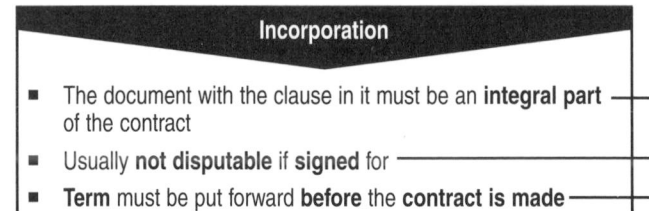

Incorporation	Case box
■ The document with the clause in it must be an **integral part** of the contract	■ *Chapelton v Barry UDC 1940*
	■ *Thompson v LMS Railway 1930*
■ Usually **not disputable** if **signed** for	■ *L'Estrange v Graucob 1934*
■ **Term** must be put forward **before** the **contract is made**	■ *Olley v Marlborough Court 1949*

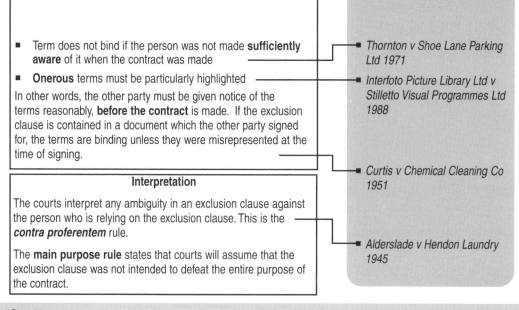

- Term does not bind if the person was not made **sufficiently aware** of it when the contract was made

  → *Thornton v Shoe Lane Parking Ltd 1971*

- **Onerous** terms must be particularly highlighted

  → *Interfoto Picture Library Ltd v Stilletto Visual Programmes Ltd 1988*

In other words, the other party must be given notice of the terms reasonably, **before the contract** is made. If the exclusion clause is contained in a document which the other party signed for, the terms are binding unless they were misrepresented at the time of signing.

→ *Curtis v Chemical Cleaning Co 1951*

Interpretation

The courts interpret any ambiguity in an exclusion clause against the person who is relying on the exclusion clause. This is the *contra proferentem* rule.

→ *Alderslade v Hendon Laundry 1945*

The **main purpose rule** states that courts will assume that the exclusion clause was not intended to defeat the entire purpose of the contract.

Terms and representations	Conditions, warranties and implied terms	Exclusion clauses	Unfair terms regulations

Protection offered to consumers by statute

Statute makes some clauses in contracts void, so that the courts would not be required to make the judgements which have been discussed above.

Clauses automatically void by statute

Exclusion of liability for death and personal injury caused by negligence.

Exclusion/limit of liability for loss or damage due to a defect in the good in consumer use.

Exclusion of the condition that seller has the right to sell the goods.

The key statutory protection is in the Unfair Contract Terms Act 1977.

This has been supplemented by the Unfair Terms in Consumer Contracts Regulations 1999.

Consumers

A **consumer** is a natural person who is acting for purposes which are outside their business.

In general, the terms of UCTA relate to clauses inserted into agreements by commercial concerns (businesses) who are selling to consumers. Private contracts between individuals are not so regulated.

Exemption clauses in contracts for the supply of goods

		Sale, HP, exchange and work + materials	
		Consumer transaction	Non-consumer transaction
I M P L I E D	T E R M S	Title	Void	Void
		Description	Void	Subject to reasonableness test
		Quality and suitability	Void	Subject to reasonableness test
		Sample	Void	Subject to reasonableness test

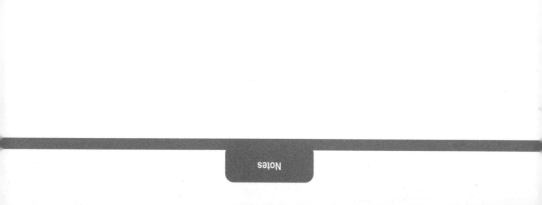

Notes

6: Breach of contract and remedies

Topic List

Breach

Damages and other common law remedies

Equitable remedies

*This chapter concentrates on when a contract is not performed properly, that is, it is **breached**. It also outlines the remedies available to the injured party. Different remedies arise under the two 'types' of law we looked at earlier, common law and equity.*

***Damages** are the most significant remedy. It is vital that you grasp the rules surrounding damages being awarded. The two-part rule of **remoteness of damage** is particularly relevant.*

repudiated = cancelled.

Breach of contract

A person is in breach of contract when they, without lawful excuse, fail to completely and exactly perform the contract.

Breach of contract creates an obligation for the person in breach to pay damages. The **obligation** to continue to **perform the contract remains**, unless:

- Defaulter is in **fundamental breach**
- Defaulter has **repudiated** the contract

Cancelled

Case box

Hochster v De La Tour 1853

White & Carter (Councils) v McGregor 1961

Repudiatory breach

Repudiation occurs where a party indicates (by words or action) that they do not intend to honour their contractual obligations.

As a result of repudiatory breach, the **injured party has a choice**. They can:

- Treat the contract as discharged so they are freed from their obligations. They may claim damages.

- Affirm the contract, perform their obligations and claim damages

Repudiatory breach is referred to as **anticipatory breach** where the party declares their intention not to perform before the date that performance is due.

Damages

Damages are a common law remedy and are primarily intended to **restore the party** who has suffered loss to the same position they would have been in **if the contract had never been performed**.

Case box

Hadley v Baxendale 1854

Victoria Laundry (Windsor) v Newman Industries 1949

Measure of damages

The measure of damages can be to cover the:

Expectation interest (to put the claimant into the position that they would have been in had the contract been performed).

Reliance interest (to compensate the claimant for wasted expenditure caused by their reliance on the contract).

The injured party is expected to **mitigate** their loss as far as reasonably possible.

There are two things for the courts to consider in relation to damages:

Remoteness of damage

The **loss must arise naturally** from the breach.

The **loss must arise in a manner** which the parties could **naturally** have **contemplated**.

Liquidated damages and penalty clauses

Calculation of damages can be complicated. Therefore some people, when negotiating contracts, pre-calculate the likely losses if the contract is breached. This saves time later.

Liquidated damages

Liquidated damages are a fixed or ascertainable sum agreed by the parties at the time of contracting, payable in the event of a breach. They must be a **genuine pre-estimate of loss**. Any sum which is not a genuine pre-estimate, but is intended to be an onerous punishment, is termed a **penalty clause**.

The key remedy for breach of contract is damages which is one of several common law remedies. There are also remedies available in equity.

Other common law remedies

Action for the price is a personal action by the person who has performed the contract to recover the sum due from the person who has breached the contract.

Quantum meruit is a restitutory award, designed to measure the value of the work that had been completed. Literally it means 'how much it is worth'.

Quantum meruit is likely to be sought when one party has already performed part of the contract when the other repudiates it.

Case box

De Barnady v Harding 1853

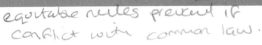

equitable rules prevail if conflict with common law.

Equitable remedies

Specific performance

An order of the court directing a person to perform their contractual obligations.

Specific performance will be ordered in instances such as the sale of land. It is **never** ordered **for personal services** such as in an employment contract.

Injunction

A discretionary court order, requiring a party to observe a negative restriction in a contract.

This can be used to enforce restraints in contracts for personal services, for example not working for others.

Rescission

This is the right to rescind voidable contracts.

This is not strictly speaking a remedy for breach of contract. It is the right of an injured party to treat the contract as never having existed.

rectification – alter document to reflect parties true intentions

Notes

7: The law of torts and professional negligence

Topic List

This chapter sets out the concept of tort, and the elements of the key tort of negligence. Negligence is particularly relevant for professional advisers, as they do not want to be sued for giving negligent advice. The three elements to a successful negligence claim are:

- *A duty of care must have existed*
- *This duty of care must have been breached*
- *The claimant was harmed as a consequence*

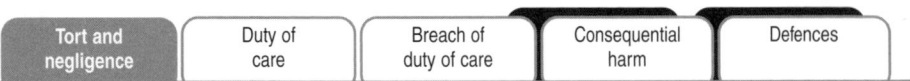
Tort

Tort is a civil wrong. The person wronged sues in a civil court for compensation. No previous relationship needs to have existed between the parties.

Negligence

Negligence 'may refer to the way in which an act is carried out' (ie carelessly). Or it refers to the tort which arises when a duty of care legally owed to a person is broken, causing loss to that person.

To succeed in an action for negligence, the claimant must prove three things, which are looked at in more detail on the following pages:

1   The defendant owed the claimant a duty of care to avoid causing damage to them or their property.

2   There was a breach of that duty by the defendant.

3   In consequence, the claimant suffered injury, damage or loss.

Case box

The concept of a duty of care stems from the case of *Donoghue v Stevenson 1932*.

The manufacturer of a drink which contained a decomposed snail was held to be liable to the person who had drunk it and become ill as a result. This was despite the fact that the drinker had not purchased the bottle, so there was no duty of care in contract.

The judge set down the principle that every person owes a duty of care to his neighbour, that is 'persons so closely and directly affected by my act that I ought to reasonably have had them in contemplation as being so affected'.

The defendant must owe the claimant a duty of care.

The doctrine has been refined since it was set out in 1932. There is now a three stage test:

1 Was the harm **reasonably foreseeable**?

2 Was there a relationship of **proximity** between the parties?

3 Considering the circumstances, is it **fair, just and reasonable** to impose a duty of care?

Case law has tended to restrict the liability of professional advisers.

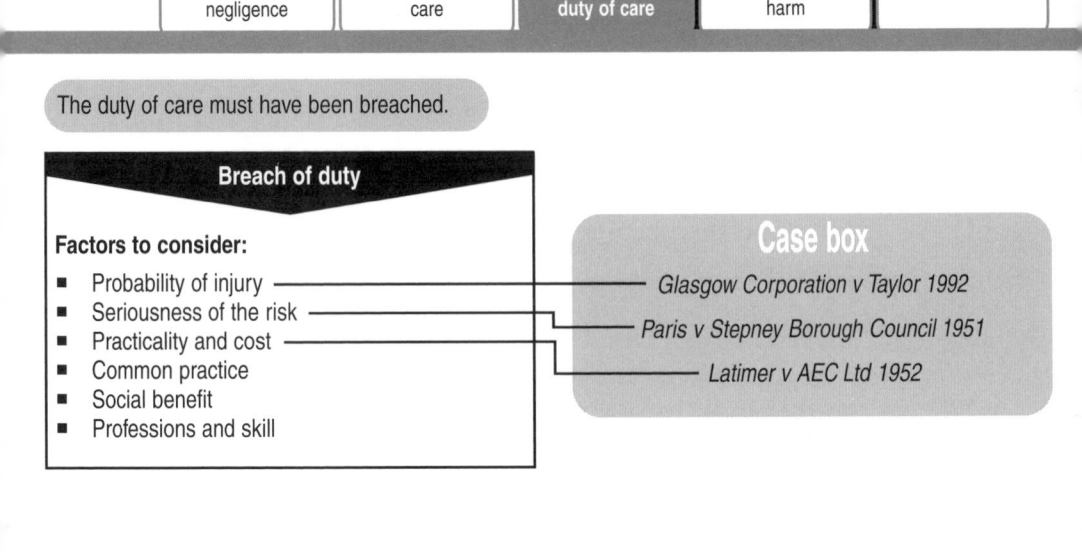

The duty of care must have been breached.

Breach of duty

Factors to consider:

- Probability of injury
- Seriousness of the risk
- Practicality and cost
- Common practice
- Social benefit
- Professions and skill

Case box

Glasgow Corporation v Taylor 1992

Paris v Stepney Borough Council 1951

Latimer v AEC Ltd 1952

Damage, loss or harm must have been suffered, **as a consequence** of the actions taken by the defendant.

The 'But for' test is used to determine causality.

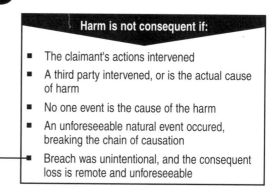

Harm is not consequent if:

- The claimant's actions intervened
- A third party intervened, or is the actual cause of harm
- No one event is the cause of the harm
- An unforeseeable natural event occured, breaking the chain of causation
- Breach was unintentional, and the consequent loss is remote and unforeseeable

Case box

The Wagon Mound 1961

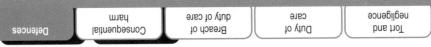

| Tort and negligence | Duty of care | Breach of duty of care | Consequential harm | Defences |

Defences to negligence

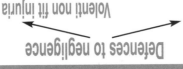

Contributory negligence

Courts may reduce the amount of damages awarded if the claimant contributed to the loss suffered.

Reductions of between 10% to 75% are usual, but 100% reduction is possible.

Sayers v Harlow UDC 1958

Volenti non fit injuria

Where the claimant voluntarily accepted the risk that caused the loss or damage, then the defendant will not be liable.

Acceptance can be **express** (such as the signing of waiver forms for dangerous sports) or **implied** (through the claimant's conduct).

ICI v Shatwell 1965

Vicarious liability

In employment situations, an employee can avoid liability for negligence if they were acting on their employer's business at the time of the incident. For the employer to be vicariously liable, the employee must have been following their employer's instructions, even if the manner of how they were carrying them out was not how the employer told them to.

Prior to 1963, liability for careless statements depended on the existence of a contractual or fiduciary relationship existing between the professional adviser and the client. There have been two important subsequent cases, setting out liability for negligent professional advice.

1 Special relationship

HB were advertising agents. HB requested information from a client's bank (HP) about the client's financial position. HP returned non-committal replies, covered by a disclaimer. The non-committal replies were held to be negligent.

HP would have been liable but for the disclaimer as they had a **special relationship** with HB, whom they knew would rely on their information.

Case box

- *Hedley Byrne & Co Ltd v Heller and Partners Ltd 1963*

Caparo Industries plc v Dickman and Others 1990

Caparo is the key case.

2 Duty to shareholders

Caparo bought shares in a company, whose audited accounts showed a profit, which in fact should have been a loss. They sued the auditors claiming that they had a duty of care to potential investors.

It was held that there was **no such duty to potential investors**, or investors increasing their stakes, only a duty to existing shareholders as a body.

Post-Caparo cases

The following cases followed Caparo and developed the law in this area.

Comments at a meeting

Verbal assurance given by an audit partner created a duty of care to a company who relied on it for a takeover.

ADT Ltd v BDO Binder Hamlyn 1995

Parent companies

Auditors owe a duty of care to parent companies when they audit their subsidiaries. This is because the report will be relied upon at group level.

Barings plc v Coopers & Lybrand 1997

Standard of care

Accountants owe a higher standard of care when advising on takeovers due to the scale of potential losses.

NRG v Bacon & Woodrow & Ernst and Young 1996

Subsidiary companies

Auditors **do not** owe a duty of care to subsidiaries when auditing the parent company's accounts as this information is not normally channelled down to them.

BCCI (Overseas) Ltd v Ernst & Whinney 1997

8: Contract of employment

Topic List

Employees and independent contractors

Terms of an employment contract

Continuity of service

Employment law can seem quite daunting, as it is a dynamic and fast growing subject. However, you are likely to be examined on some of the core elements of employment law which are summarised here.

In this chapter, focus on the key distinction between employees and independent contractors. Employees get the benefit of the protection discussed in this and the next chapter, as a general rule, independent contractors do not.

Employee

An individual who has entered into or works under a contract of employment.

Independent contractor

An individual who provides services to an entity under a contract for those services, which is not a contract of employment.

It is important to distinguish between employees and independent contractors. The courts will look at the reality of the situation and then apply three tests to determine whether someone has a contract of employment or a contract for services.

Reality of the situation

What the parties say is less conclusive than the reality of the situation. → *Ferguson v John Dawson & Partners 1976*

If there is doubt as to the nature of the relationship, the courts will look → *Massey v Crown Life Assurance 1978*
at the agreement between the parties.

Case box

Agency workers

The status of agency workers may be determined by:

- **Length of service** – *Frank v Reuters Ltd 2003*
- **Control (client or agency)** – *Motorola v Davidson and Melville Craig 2001*

Tests applied by the courts

Control test: Has the employer control over the way in which the employee performs their duties?

Integration test: If the employee is so skilled that they cannot be controlled, are they integrated into the organisation?

Multiple (economic reality) test: Is the employee really working on their own account?

Case box

■ *Mersey Docks & Harbour Board v Coggins & Griffiths (Liverpool) 1947*

■ *Cassidy v Ministry of Health 1951*

■ *Ready Mixed Concrete (South East) v Ministry of Pensions & National Insurance 1968*

Significant factors

- Does the employee use their own **tools and equipment,** or does the employer provide?
- Does the employer have the right to **choose and dismiss employees**?
- Payment of **salary** is a fair indication that the individual is an employee.
- Working for a number of **different people** is not necessarily a sign of self-employment.

8: Contract of employment

Importance of the distinction

FACTOR	EMPLOYEE	INDEPENDENT CONTRACTOR (IC)
Tax/social security	Class 1 NI Deductions under PAYE	Class 2 and 4 NI Accounts for tax to HMRC
Legal protection	Substantial employment law	Less protection (normal contract law)
Contractual rights	A number of rights and duties are implied into contracts of employment	Rights and duties do not extend to a contract for services
VAT	Irrelevant to employees	May need to register for VAT
Bankruptcy	Employee has preferential rights as a creditor	IC would be a standard creditor, therefore get paid later
Health and Safety	There is significant common law and statutory protection	In practice the protection extends to ICs and employees

You have already learnt the key legal rules about the formation of contract, and the basic elements of a contract of employment are no different.

A contract of employment may be written, oral or a mixture of the two. However, some **written particulars** are required. Within two months of starting the employer must give written particulars to the employee, including:

- **Names** of the **employer** and the **employee**
- The **date** on which the employment began
- Details relating to **continuous service**
- **Pay-scale** or rate and intervals at which the employee is to be paid
- **Hours of work**, including any specified normal working hours
- Any **holiday** and **holiday pay** entitlement
- **Sick leave** and **sick pay** entitlement
- **Pensions** and pension schemes
- Length of **notice** of termination to be given on each side
- The **title** of the job which the employee is employed to do

Common law duties

There is an overriding duty of mutual trust and confidence between the employer and the employee.

Most of these common law duties are also contained within/augmented by statutory implied terms.

Other common law duties of the **employer** include:

- To pay **reasonable remuneration** to employees
- To **indemnify the employee** for expenses/losses incurred in the course of employment
- To take care of the employee's **health and safety** while at work
- To **provide work**, ONLY where
  - Employee is an apprentice
  - Employee is paid on the basis of work done
  - Opportunity to work is the essence of the contract

Employee

The employee has a fundamental duty of faithful service to the employer, from which all their other duties arise.

- **Reasonable competence** to do their job

- **Obedience** to the employer's instructions unless they require them to act unlawfully or expose themselves to danger

- Duty to **account for all money and property** received during the course of employment

- **Reasonable skill and care** in the performance of their work

- **Personal service** (they may not delegate their work)

Case box

Hivac Ltd v Park Royal Scientific Instruments Ltd 1946

Pepper v Webb 1969

Boston Deep Sea Fishing and Ice Co v Ansell 1888

Terms implied by statute

A variety of terms are implied into contracts of employment by statute. Key legislation includes:

- Employment Rights Act 1996
- National Minimum Wage Act 1998
- Employment Act 2002
- Equality Act 2010

Pay

Everyone is entitled to at least the national minimum wage. NMWA98. The amount is updated annually.

Time off work

An employee is entitled to time off work in various circumstances:

- Trade union duties and activities
- Looking for work if made redundant
- Certain public duties
- Ante-natal care

ERA96

Equality

Employees have protection against discrimination, harrassment or victimisation on the basis of their (amongst others) age, sex, race, religion and sexuality. EA10

Justification test

Discrimination judgements are viewed in light of a single justification test. This means employers must prove their actions were a **proportionate means** of achieving a **legitimate aim**.

Health and safety

An employer has a duty to ensure, as far as is reasonably practicable, the health and safety of persons at work. HSWA74

Under the **Enterprise and Regulatory Reform Act 2013**, employers are only liable to pay compensation to employees injured at work if they are found to have acted negligently. Employees are not entitled to compensation if their employer has taken all reasonable steps to prevent injury.

Parental leave

Every woman has a right to maternity leave and some are entitled to maternity pay. There is also a right to return to work. ERA96/99 Fathers are also entitled to paternity leave and pay. EA02

Working time

A worker's average working time per week in a 17 week period should not exceed 48 hours/7 days.
WTR98

Key

EA02	Employment Act 2002
ERA96	Employment Rights Act 1996
ERA99	Employment Relations Act 1999
HWSA74	Health and Safety at Work Act 1974
NMWA98	National Minimum Wage Act 1998
WTR98	Working Time Regulations 1998
EA10	Equality Act 2010

Flexible working

Employees have the right to request changes to their time, hours and place of work if they meet certain criteria.

Employers may only refuse a request on specific grounds.
EA02

Varying the terms of an employment contract

Consent might be demonstrated by oral agreement, signing a statement of new terms or by showing acceptance by working under the new terms.

A **change** in contract terms can **only** be made with the **consent** of **both** the parties.

Employees and
independent contractors

Terms of an
employment contract

Continuity
of service

Continuity of service

There are detailed rules about what constitutes continuous service. It is most important to grasp the general rule and learn the exceptions to it.

Much of the statutory employment protection is only available to employees with one year's **continuous service**.

Transfer of undertakings

When a business in the UK is 'transferred', the employees are also transferred with unbroken continuous service. It applies where there is a real change of ownership and continuity in the business, for example, where one company takes over another.

9: Dismissal and redundancy

Topic List

Notice and termination of contract by breach

Employment tribunals

Wrongful dismissal

Unfair dismissal

Redundancy

You must be clear on the issues surrounding unfair dismissal:

- *Criteria for claiming it*
- *Automatically fair/unfair reasons for dismissal*
- *Employer reasonableness*

Unfair dismissal is important because of the high level of compensation available. However, remember that a highly paid employee might seek wrongful dismissal instead as damages could be worth more than the maximum statutory compensation for unfair dismissal.

Notice must not be less than the statutory minimum. It may be given without specific reason unless the contract states otherwise.

Notice period required depends on the length of the employee's continuous service:

Continuously employed > one month but < two years. One week's notice required

Continuously employed > two years but < 12 years. One week per year employed

Continuously employed > 12 years. No less than twelve weeks notice required

Termination of contract by breach

An employment contract is terminated by breach in four situations:

- Summary dismissal
- Constructive dismissal
- Employer unable to continue
- Employee repudiates contract

Both examples of dismissal without proper notice. A dismissal is generally held to be lawful if there was proper notice, unless it is later found to be wrongful/unfair.

Constructive dismissal

Constructive dismissal occurs where the employer, although willing to carry on the contract, repudiates some essential term (eg changing the employee's duties) which causes the employee to resign.

Employment tribunals

Employment tribunals have jurisdiction to deal with all manner of employment related disputes such as wrongful and unfair dismissal and redundancy, which formerly had to be heard in the civil courts. The Employment Tribunals (Constitution and Rules of Procedure) Regulations 2013 apply to them.

The objective of an employment tribunal is to resolve **employment disputes**. A hearing is normally convened with an Employment Judge and two other individuals. Each side makes its case and a decision is made. In some cases, the parties will be encouraged to settle their dispute informally through **mediation**.

Settlement agreements and early conciliation

The **Enterprise and Regulatory Reform Act 2013** aims to reduce the number of employment disputes that go to tribunal to save the cost and time involved in them. The Act allows employers and employees to use settlement agreements to part company on agreed terms.

The Act also requires employees to contact **ACAS** (the Government-sponsored organisation that aims to prevent and resolve employment disputes) before filing a claim at an employment tribunal. This allows the parties to resolve the situation before incurring the expense of going to tribunal.

Wrongful dismissal

Wrongful dismissal is a common law concept arising in specific circumstances, giving an employee an action for breach of contract. For example, where insufficient notice has been given.

Therefore, where an employee has been summarily dismissed, there may be a claim for damages at common law.

The only **effective remedy** for wrongful dismissal is generally **damages, based on loss of earnings**. These can be awarded in the civil courts or an employment tribunal.

The wronged party is expected to **mitigate** their loss, for example, by seeking other work.

Justifiable reasons for dismissal

- Wilful disobedience of a lawful order
- Misconduct
- Dishonesty (where the employee is in a position of particular trust)
- Incompetence or neglect, where an employee fails to use the skills they claim to have
- Gross negligence, depending on the nature of the job
- Immorality (if it will affect the performance of duties/reputation of the business)
- Drunkenness (in aggravated circumstances or repeated)

Unfair dismissal

Unfair dismissal is a statutory concept. As a rule, every employee has the right not to be unfairly dismissed. The distinction between unfair and wrongful dismissal is primarily in the remedies available.

The remedy for unfair dismissal is generally compensation.

Applying for unfair dismissal

Step one Employee applies to tribunal, showing they are a dismissed, qualifying employee

Step two Employer has to show main reason for dismissal

Employer has to show that they acted reasonably

Criteria for seeking remedies for unfair dismissal

- **Continuously employed** for more than two years
- Have been **dismissed** (this includes constructive dismissal)
- Have been **unfairly** dismissed (for the tribunal to decide)

Justification of dismissal

Justifiable reasons for dismissal

- Want of **capability or qualifications** on the part of the employee

- **Misconduct** of the employee (there is a distinction between gross/ordinary)

- **Redundancy**

- **Legal prohibition or restriction** meaning that the employee could not work

- **Other substantial reason** justifying dismissal. For example, employee married a competitor, or didn't accept a reorganisation

Employer reasonableness

The tribunal must ensure the employer has acted reasonably.

The employer is expected to follow disciplinary procedures and give warnings.

- Has the correct procedure been applied?
- Did the employer account for all circumstances?
- What would a reasonable employer have done?

Automatically unfair reasons for dismissal

- Pregnancy
- Spent conviction
- Trade union membership
- On transfer of undertakings
- Taking steps to avert health and safety problems
- Exercising certain rights such as under minimum wage, working time or Sunday trading regulations or public interest disclosure acts

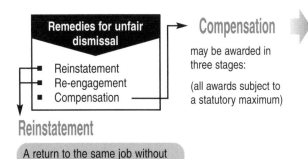

Reinstatement

A return to the same job without any break of continuity.

Re-engagement

The employee is given new employment with the employer on terms specified in the order. In practice, such solutions are rare.

Compensation

may be awarded in three stages:

(all awards subject to a statutory maximum)

Basic award	
41+ years	1½ week's pay for each year of service (max 20)
22–40 years	1 week's pay for each year of service (max 20)
21 years and under	½ week's pay for each year of service.
Compensatory award	
Any age	For any additional loss of earnings, expenses and benefits on common law principles of damages for breach of contract.
Punitive award	
Any age	26–52 weeks pay (if employer fails to comply with the tribunal's orders)

Redundancy

A dismissal is treated as redundancy if the only or main reason is:

- The employer has ceased, or intends to cease, to carry on the business in which the employee has worked.

- The requirements of that business for employees to carry on the work done by the employee have ceased or diminished.

Entitlement to redundancy payments

- Employees must have **two years** continuous service.

- The employer may make an employee an offer of **alternative employment.** If the employee refuses the alternative employment, they lose their right to redundancy payments.

- An employee who has been dismissed for **misconduct** is not entitled to redundancy pay even though they may become redundant.

- An employee's remuneration may depend on provision of work. When an employee is '**laid off**' or '**kept on short time**' they may claim redundancy by informing the employer of their intention to do so.

- Payments must be claimed within **six months**.

Calculation of payment

Redundancy pay is calculated in the same way as the unfair dismissal basic award.

10: Agency law

Topic List

Creation of agency

Authority of the agent

Relations with third parties (3P)

Agency is an important area of the syllabus because it contributes to your understanding of:

- *Partnerships*
- *Promoters*
- *Directors' duties*

Agency

A relationship which exists between two legal persons (principal and agent) in which the function of the agent is to form a contract between the principal and a third party.

Example

P asks A to take P's shoes to be mended. P has expressly asked A to be his agent for the purposes of making that contract with the shoe repairer.

Agency may be **created** by:

Agreement

- **Express**

  Agent is expressly appointed by the principal (as in the example above)

- **Implied**

  Two persons imply such a relationship by their conduct

Types of agent

- Partners
- Directors
- Auctioneers
- Brokers
- Promoters
- Factors
- Commercial agents

Ratification

A principal can ratify the actions of another to create an agency relationship after the event.

Principal must:

- Exist when the contract is made
- Have legal capacity at that time
- Ratify within a reasonable time
- Ratify the whole contract
- Communicate ratification clearly

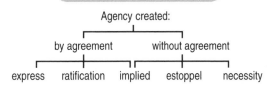

Agent of necessity

Where a person who, when faced with an emergency situation, intervenes on behalf of another.

Agency created:

by agreement — without agreement

express   ratification   implied   estoppel   necessity

Estoppel

Where a principal holds out to a thrid party (3P) that a person is their agent, they are estopped from denying the agent's authority. This is **agency by estoppel**.

The contract made by the agent is binding on the principal and the 3P only if the agent was acting within the limits of their authority from the principal.

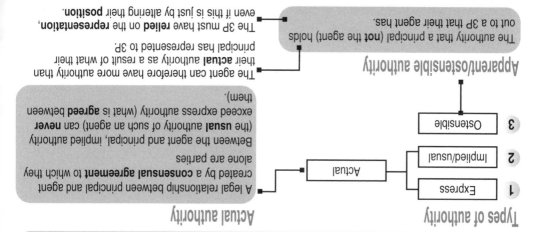

Types of authority

Actual authority

A legal relationship between principal and agent created by a **consensual agreement** to which they alone are parties

Between the agent and principal, implied authority (the **usual** authority of such an agent) can **never** exceed express authority (what is **agreed** between them).

Actual	1	Express
	2	Implied/usual
	3	Ostensible

Apparent/ostensible authority

The authority that a principal (**not** the agent) holds out to a 3P that their agent has.

The agent can therefore have more authority than their **actual** authority as a result of what their principal has represented to 3P.

The 3P must have **relied** on the **representation**, even if this is just by altering their **position**.

Principal

The principal is liable to the 3P for contracts formed by an agent within their actual or ostensible authority.

Agent

An agent generally has no liability on the contract and is not entitled to enforce it.

Exceptions:

- Agent intended to take personal liability
- Usual business practice for agent to be liable
- Agent is contracting on his own behalf, not for a principal

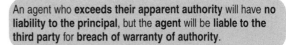

An agent who **exceeds their apparent authority** will have **no liability to the principal**, but the **agent will be liable to the third party** for **breach of warranty of authority**.

Notes

11: Partnerships

In this chapter we consider the concept of a partnership and the important issue of partners' liability.

Limited Liability Partnerships (LLPs) are an important form of partnership for professionals such as accountants.

Partnerships

The relation which subsists between **persons** carrying on a **business** in **common** with a view of **profit**

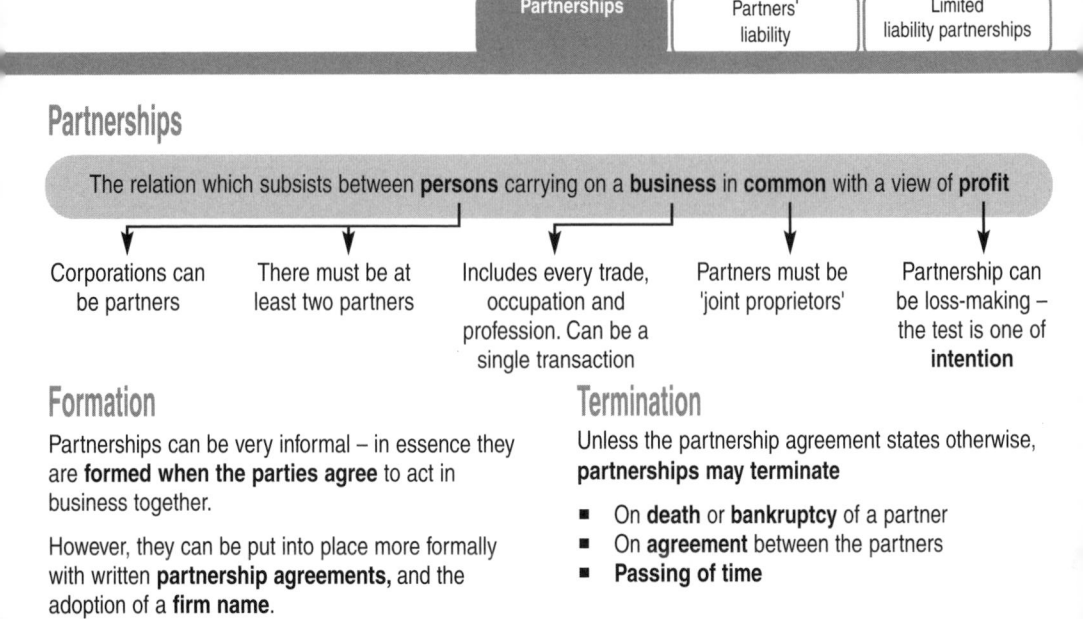

Corporations can be partners

There must be at least two partners

Includes every trade, occupation and profession. Can be a single transaction

Partners must be 'joint proprietors'

Partnership can be loss-making – the test is one of **intention**

Formation

Partnerships can be very informal – in essence they are **formed when the parties agree** to act in business together.

However, they can be put into place more formally with written **partnership agreements,** and the adoption of a **firm name**.

Termination

Unless the partnership agreement states otherwise, **partnerships may terminate**

- On **death** or **bankruptcy** of a partner
- On **agreement** between the partners
- **Passing of time**

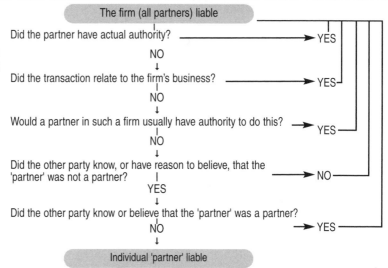

Partners' liability

Partners are liable for each other's acts under the rules of agency. The rules are summarised again to the right in this context.

New partners: Liable for debts incurred after they became a partner ONLY.

Retiring partners: Continue to be liable for debts unless they have given notice of retirement to each creditor.

The firm (all partners) liable

Did the partner have actual authority? ⟶ YES

NO
↓

Did the transaction relate to the firm's business? ⟶ YES

NO
↓

Would a partner in such a firm usually have authority to do this? ⟶ YES

NO
↓

Did the other party know, or have reason to believe, that the 'partner' was not a partner? ⟶ NO

YES
↓

Did the other party know or believe that the 'partner' was a partner? ⟶ YES

NO
↓

Individual 'partner' liable

Limited Liability Partnerships

An 'LLP' is a cross between a company and a partnership. Crucially, partners have limited liability, so LLPs are more regulated than partnerships.

To be incorporated, the subscribers to the LLP must file the following details with the Registrar of Companies:

- The **name** of the LLP
- The **location** of its registered office (in England and Wales, or in Scotland) and its address
- The **names and addresses** of all LLP's members
- Who the **designated members** are (who take responsibility for the LLP's publicity requirements).

With regard to publicity, the LLP's designated members must:

- **File** certain notices with the Registrar, such as when a member leaves
- **Sign and file accounts**
- Appoint **auditors** if appropriate

Every member-partner is treated as an agent of the partnership (just like a director of a company) and therefore can bind the LLP by their actions.

12: Corporations and legal personality

Topic List

Sole traders and legal identity

Company liability

Types of company

Veil of incorporation

Distinction between companies and partnerships

In this chapter it is important to get to grips with:

- *The essential features of a company*
- *The distinction between companies and partnerships*

Understanding the features of a company will aid your understanding of the rest of company law.

Sole traders

Sole traders own and run businesses which are not legally distinct from the owner.

Companies

Companies are legal entities, separate from the natural persons connected with them, for example, their members.

Legal status of sole traders

No formality

Independence and self-accountability

Personal supervision

All profits accrue to owner

Owner's wealth at risk

Corporate legal personality

The law recognises a company is a distinct legal person.

The company is liable for its debts and has its own rights and obligations.

Liability of a company and its members

Case box

Salomon v Salomon and Co Ltd 1897

Lee v Lee's Air Farming Ltd 1960

The Salomon case established that a company is a legal entity separate from its owners.

The fact that a company is a separate legal entity gives rise to many of its characteristics.

The most important characteristic is limited liability for the members of the company.

Key points to remember:

- The **company** is **liable without limit** for its own debts.

- **Members** of the company do not have to pay the debts of the company if it fails.

- **Members** will have to pay any money still owed from purchasing their shares, or under a guarantee.

Limited

- Can be limited by shares/guarantee
- Members' liability limited only (not company's)
- Two types: private and public

Public

- May offer securities to the public
- Minimum share capital £50,000
- Minimum one member/two directors
- Name must end with plc
- Must have a trading certificate to trade

Private

- May not offer securities to the public
- No minimum capital requirement
- Minimum one member/one director
- Name must end with word Limited/Ltd

Unlimited

- Members have unlimited liability
- Can only ever be a private company
- Reduced disclosure and may purchase shares from members easily

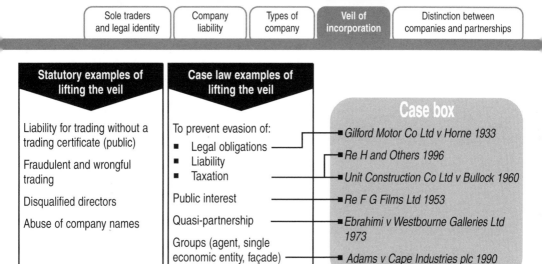

Statutory examples of lifting the veil

Liability for trading without a trading certificate (public)

Fraudulent and wrongful trading

Disqualified directors

Abuse of company names

Case law examples of lifting the veil

To prevent evasion of:
- Legal obligations
- Liability
- Taxation

Public interest

Quasi-partnership

Groups (agent, single economic entity, façade)

Case box

- *Gilford Motor Co Ltd v Horne 1933*
- *Re H and Others 1996*
- *Unit Construction Co Ltd v Bullock 1960*
- *Re F G Films Ltd 1953*
- *Ebrahimi v Westbourne Galleries Ltd 1973*
- *Adams v Cape Industries plc 1990*

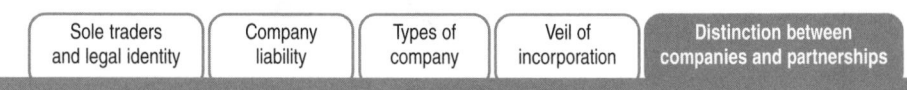

Distinction between companies and partnerships

Companies	Partnerships
■ Separate legal entity to members	■ No existence beyond members
■ Members' liability usually limited	■ Partners' liability usually unlimited
■ May have any number of members (at least one)	■ May be limited to 20 partners (not professional practices). At least two
■ Perpetual succession	■ Partnership dissolves when a partner leaves
■ Members own transferable shares	■ Partners cannot assign their interest
■ The company owns its assets	■ Partners own assets jointly
■ Company must have at least one director (two for a public company)	■ Every partner may participate in management
■ Must have a written constitution	■ May have written partnership agreement (not required)
■ Must usually file accounts with Registrar	■ Does not have to file accounts
■ May offer security of a floating charge over assets	■ May not create a floating charge over assets
■ Strict rules over repayment of capital	■ Partners may withdraw capital easily

13: Company formation

Topic List

Promoters and pre-incorporation contracts

Registration procedures and commencement of business

Statutory registers

Accounts and returns

In this chapter we consider how companies are formed and how contracts made by those forming the company are treated by the law.

It is important to understand the obligations of a company to file accounts and returns as well as to keep specific company registers.

A company promoter

A person who undertakes to form a company for a specified purpose and takes the necessary steps to create it. Those who act solely in a professional capacity are not promoters.

Duties of promoters

General duty of **reasonable skill and care.**

Fiduciary duty to those people who are to own the company (if different from themselves). This includes the following duties of an agent:

- Disclosure of interests
- Not to make a wrongful profit
- Avoidance of conflict of interests

Wrongful profits can be recovered; sometimes contracts may be rescinded.

A pre-incorporation contract

A pre-incorporation contract is a contract purported to be made by a company or its agent at a time **before the company has received its certificate of incorporation.**

Liabilities of promoters

The company is **not bound** by pre-incorporation contracts.

Promoters are personally liable on pre-incorporation contracts.

Pre-incorporation expenses cannot automatically be recovered by a promoter, but once formed, the company may agree reimbursement.

Registration procedures

A company is formed when the Registrar issues it a **certificate of incorporation**. This states its name, registered number, the liability of its members, and whether it is public or private.

To obtain a certificate of incorporation, the promoters of a company send the Registrar:

Memorandum of association	The memorandum should be signed by the subscribers. Each subscriber agrees to become a member and to subscribe for at least one share.
Articles of association (if not default model articles)	Articles are signed by the same subscriber(s), dated and witnessed. Default model articles, relevant to the type of company formed, become the company's articles if no articles are sent to the Registrar.
Statement of proposed officers	The statement gives the particulars of the first director(s) and secretary (if applicable). They must consent to act in this capacity.
Statement of compliance	The statement that the requirements of the Companies Act in respect of registration have been complied with.
Statement of capital	A Statement of Capital and Initial Shareholdings must be completed by all companies to be limited by shares.
Registration fee	A registration fee is payable on application.

Off-the-shelf companies

The alternative way of setting up a company is to buy a company which has already been registered. This is called buying a company 'off the shelf'.

Advantages	Disadvantages
☑ The application and the following documents are already filed: – Memo and articles – Fee – Statements of proposed officers, compliance and capital ☑ No risk of liability arising on pre-incorporation contracts	☒ Directors may want to amend the articles (usually default model articles provided) ☒ May need to change the name ☒ Need to transfer subscriber shares

Commencement of business

Private company: may commence business from the date of incorporation as stated on the certificate of incorporation.

Public company: must obtain a trading certificate from the Registrar before it is allowed to trade.

The key source of information on a UK company is its file at **Companies' House**.

Companies are also required by law to keep a number of **registers**, **records** and **returns**.

They must be kept at the company's **registered office** or another registered place known as a **Single Alternative Inspection Location** (SAIL)

Statutory registers

Register

Register of members

Register of charges

Register of directors and secretaries

Records of directors' service contracts and indemnities

Records of resolutions and meetings of the company

Register of debentureholders

Register of disclosed interests in shares (public company ONLY)

A register of **directors' residential addresses** must be kept by the company although it is not available to the public.

In the register of directors a director may provide a **service address** instead of their residential address.

Annual accounts

The directors must for each accounting period:

- Prepare a balance sheet and profit and loss account giving a true and fair view
- Lay those accounts and a directors' report before the general meeting of shareholders (public companies only)
- Deliver a copy of those accounts (often in abbreviated form) to the Registrar to be put on the company's file

Accounting records

The directors are required to keep accounting records which show the company's financial position at any given time. They should include:

- Daily entries of sums paid and received
- A record of assets and liabilities
- Statements of stock held at the end of each financial year
- Statements of stocktaking to back up the above
- Statements of goods bought and sold (except retail sales)

Annual return

The company must send a return to the Registrar annually giving details of directors, secretary and shares.

14: Constitution of a company

Topic List

A company's constitution

Company objects and capacity

The constitution as a contract

Company name

Under the Companies Act 2006, a company's constitution comprises its articles of association as amended by any resolutions or agreements that it makes.

A company's objects describe the activities it may take part in. For most companies they are unlimited but in some companies they may be restricted. It is important to understand the implications of breaching the objects.

The Memorandum of Association

The historic document which states that the founders (the subscribers) wish to form a company and agree to become a member, taking at least one share each.

The Articles of Association

The articles provide the basis of a company's constitution. They define the rules and regulations governing the management of the affairs of the company, the rights of the members and the powers of the directors.

Content of articles

- Appointment and dismissal of directors
- Powers, responsibilities and liabilities of directors
- Directors' meetings
- Administering general meetings
- Members' rights

- Dividends
- Communication with members
- Class meetings
- Issue of shares
- Transfer of shares
- Documents and records
- Company secretary

A company may adopt all or part of the relevant statutory **model articles**. These contain all the items mentioned here.

Model Articles

Where a company fails to register articles, it will be automatically given **default model articles** relevant to the type of company formed.

Companies may also choose to adopt model articles and amend them if they wish by special resolution.

Alterability

The articles may be amended by a **special resolution** or a **written resolution** with a **75% majority**. However, alterability can be reduced by:

1 Providing members with additional notes so they can block an alteration.

2 Requiring a particular member to be present for a quorum to exist. The member may prevent the meeting from being held by absenting themselves.

3 'Entrenching' provisions in the articles. This means specific articles can only be amended or removed if certain conditions (that are more restrictive than a special resolution) are met. Provisions cannot be drafted so they can **never** be altered.

Restrictions on alteration

- Alterations may not **conflict** with the Companies Act.

- Members may not be **compelled** to subscribe for additional shares or to accept increased liability for shares already held.

- Certain alterations require the correct **rights variation procedure** to have been followed.

- Alterations cannot **remove rights** already acquired by performing a contract.

- A person whose **contract is contained** in the articles cannot prevent it from being altered.

- All alterations are void if the majority who approve them are not acting *bona fide* in the interest of the company as a whole.

Company objects

Historically, a company's objects clause stated the activities which a company intends to follow.

Under the Companies Act 2006 a company has unrestricted objects. This means it can carry out any lawful activity.

Companies may pass a special resolution (75% majority) to introduce restrictions into a company's objects.

Ultra vires

Where a company acts in contravention of any restrictions placed on the objects, the actions are deemed *ultra vires*.

Statutory third party protection re *ultra vires*

Sections 39 and 40 of the Companies Act 2006 give security to commercial transactions for third parties, so they can enforce an *ultra vires* contract.

Where a **third party** deals with a company in good faith, but the contract is *ultra vires* for the company, the company cannot argue that the third party should have known that the contract was *ultra vires*. Third parties are not required to enquire whether or not the objects are restricted and can enforce the contract in such circumstances.

The *ultra vires* rule still works **internally** between the company and its members. *Ultra vires* transactions with a director, or in connection with a director, are voidable at the instance of the company. Such people are deemed to know they are *ultra vires*.

The constitution as a contract

Members to company/company to members

The articles bind members to the company.

- In their capacity as **members**
- Not in any other capacity (eg member is company solicitor)

Members to members

The articles bind the members to each other.

Supplement to other contracts

If any outsider makes a separate contract with the company which is silent on a point covered in the articles, the **articles can form part of the contract** on that specific point.

Case box

- *Hickman v Kent or Romney Marsh Sheepbreeders Association 1915*

- *Eley v Positive Government Security Life Assurance Co 1876*

- *Rayfield v Hands 1958*

Statutory rules on company names

- Must end Ltd (limited) or plc (public limited company) where relevant.

- May not have same name as another company on the register (incidental words are ignored).

- May not be 'offensive', 'sensitive' or criminal.

- Official approval is required for words which suggest an official connection.

- May omit 'Ltd' if it is a private company limited by shares or guarantee licensed before 25/02/82 whose objects are to promote commerce, art, science, education, religion or charity and assets are spent promoting them.

Passing off

A company which believes its rights have been infringed may apply for an injunction to restrain another from using a name.

If it causes confusion in the eyes of consumers

- Unless businesses are different
- Or exclusive word has general use

Case box

Ewing v Buttercup Margarine Co Ltd 1917

A company can also **appeal to the Company Names Adjudicators** under the Companies Act 2006.

15: Share capital

Topic List

Shares and capital

Class rights

Issuing shares

*It is vital that you master the different types of share, and the characteristics/implications of a share as opposed to a debenture. The **key** issue is that a shareholder is a member of the company, rather than a creditor.*

Share capital

A share is the interest of a shareholder in the company measured by a sum of money, for the purposes of a liability in the first place, and of interest in the second, but also consisting of a series of mutual covenants entered into by all the shareholders.

- It must be **paid for** (liability)
- It gives **entitlement** to **dividends** and **return of capital** (interest)
- It is a **bargain with other shareholders** (mutual covenants)

The term **capital** is used in several senses in company legislation.

Loan capital

Loan capital consists of debentures or other long-term loans.

Issued and allotted share capital

Issued share capital is the type, class, number and amount of shares issued and **allotted** to specific shareholders.

Called/paid up share capital

Called up share capital is the amount which the company has required shareholders to pay on the shares issued. **Paid up share capital** is the amount which shareholders have actually paid on the shares issued and called-up.

Equity share capital

Equity share capital is a company's issued share capital less capital which carries preferential rights. Equity share capital normally comprises ordinary shares.

Preference shares

Preference shares carry a **fixed rate** of **dividend**, paid **in priority** to any other dividend.

Rights of preference shareholders

- The right to a dividend is usually cumulative, and does not mean the dividend must be paid annually
- In liquidation, holders are usually entitled to unpaid dividend arrears
- There is no entitlement to participate in dividends above the fixed rate

Ordinary shares

Ordinary shares entitle the holder to a company's remaining divisible profits and assets after prior investors (creditors and preference shareholders) have been paid in a liquidation.

Redeemable shares

Redeemable shares are shares issued by the company that it is entitled to re-purchase at a later date.

Treasury shares

These are created when a company legitimately purchases its own shares for cash or out of distributable profit. The company can re-issue these shares without the usual formalities.

Companies have discretion to issue shares which have **special rights attached** to them. For example regarding **dividends, return of capital** in winding up, **voting** and **appointment** of **directors**.

Variation of class rights

Variation of class rights involves an **alteration** of the **position of shareholders** with regard to those benefits or duties which they have by virtue of their shares.

Such a variation can only be made by the consent of:

- The holders of the shares
- A majority specified in the articles

The standard procedure for a variation of class rights is a **special resolution** (75% majority) cast at a separate meeting of the holders or by **written consent.**

Minority rights

A minority of holders of the class of share may appeal to the court about a variation if they:

- Together hold > 15% of relevant shares
- Have not consented to the variation
- Apply to the court within 21 days

In order to be successful, the minority have to show that the majority was seeking advantage as a different class.

When variation rights do not apply

- Issuing shares in the class to others
- Subdividing other classes of shares
- Returning capital to preference shareholders
- Creating/issuing new forms of preference share

Directors' power to allot

Public companies and private companies with > one class of share:

Power given by members or general authority to allot

Private companies with one class of share:

Directors have authority to allot unless restricted by the articles.

Value of shares

Shares have a nominal value and **must not be issued at a discount** to that value. They can be issued at a premium to the nominal value.

Pre-emption rights

Pre-emption rights are the rights of existing shareholders to be offered any new issues of ordinary shares *pro rata* to their existing holding.

There is generally **a statutory duty** for companies to offer new issues of shares to existing shareholders first, in proportion to their current holdings. This means that their **voting power does not become diluted** by the issue.

A private company may **permanently exclude pre-emption rights** in its articles. **Any company may disapply pre-emption rights** by special resolution (75% majority) for individual issues.

Rights issues

A rights issue is a right given to shareholders to subscribe for further shares in the company, usually pro-rata to their existing shareholding.

Bonus issues

A bonus issue is the capitalisation of the reserves of a company by the issue of additional shares to existing shareholders in proportion to their shareholdings – usually fully paid up.

Issuing shares at premium

Shares may be issued at a premium to their nominal value but **never at a discount**.

Consideration for shares

At least the nominal value of the shares, plus the whole of any premium, must be obtained in money or money's worth (cash or non-cash).

Share premium account

When shares are issued at a premium, the premium is accounted for in the share premium account. Uses of share premium account:

- To create fully paid shares under a bonus issue
- To pay issue costs and commission in respect of a new share issue

Notes

16: Loan capital

Topic List

Borrowing and loan capital

Charges

Debentureholders' remedies

The topics in this chapter are prime examination topics. You could be asked to identify the differences between shares and debentures, or fixed and floating charges. It is therefore an important chapter to get to grips with and to practise questions on.

All companies formed under the Companies Act 2006 have **implied borrowing powers** for purposes incidental to the trade or business. There is usually a maximum borrowing power given to directors contained in the articles. Even if the directors breach this power the lender still has rights to enforce it.

Loan capital

All long-term borrowing:

- Permanent overdrafts
- Secured and unsecured loans

Debentures

Written acknowledgments of debt by a company, usually referring to interest/terms of repayment. May be secured on company assets.

Debenture trust deed

- Trustee appointed for prospective holders of debenture stock
- Nominal amount and repayment details defined
- Company enters covenants, eg about secured assets

Advantages of debenture trust deed

The key advantage is that a body of debenture stock holders are represented by one trustee.

- ☑ Trustee intervenes in default
- ☑ Trustee can consult all holders and seek agreement
- ☑ Security can be legal mortgage

Rights of debentureholders

Although both own transferable company securities, it is helpful to contrast the rights of debentureholders with those of shareholders.

Factor	Shareholder	Debentureholder
Role	Is a proprietor or **owner** of the company	Is a **creditor** of the company
Voting rights	May vote at general meetings	May not vote
Cost of investment	Shares **may not** be issued at a discount	Debentures **may** be offered at a discount
Return	Dividends only paid from distributable profits when directors declare them	Interest **must** be paid when it is due
Redemption	Statutory restrictions on redeeming shares	No restriction on redeeming debentures
Liquidation	Shareholders are the last people to be paid in a winding up	Debentures must be paid back before shares

Advantages of debentures

- ☑ Easily traded

- ☑ Terms clear and specific

- ☑ Assets under a floating charge may be traded

- ☑ Popular due to guaranteed income

- ☑ Interest tax-deductible by company

- ☑ No restrictions on issue or redemption by a company

Disadvantages of debentures

- ☒ May have to pay high interest rates to make them attractive

- ☒ Interest payments mandatory

- ☒ Interest payments to debentureholders may upset shareholders if dividends fall

- ☒ Debentureholders' remedies of appointing liquidators or receivers may be disastrous for the company

- ☒ Crystallisation of a floating charge can cause trading difficulties for a company

Charges

A charge is security over company assets which is given to a lender. It is often given in the form of a legal mortgage and gives the lender rights over the assets. **Charges must be registered to be valid.** However, the debt is still valid even if the charge is not registered.

Fixed charges

A fixed charge is given to secured creditors relating to specific assets of the company. It gives the holder the right of enforcement against that specific asset. It ranks first in order of priority in liquidation.

Floating charge

A floating charge is given on a class of assets which changes all the time due to its nature (eg stock). The assets may be used in the course of business until the holder enforces the charge.

Priority of charges

- Fixed and floating charges must be registered within 21 days of creation to be valid and enforceable.
- Fixed charges always rank ahead of floating charges regardless of date of creation unless the fixed charge holder had notice of the floating charge when the fixed charge was created.
- Fixed charges on the same asset rank according to date of creation.
- Floating charges on the same asset rank according to date of creation.

16: Loan capital

Floating charges **crystallise** (become fixed) in certain situations:

- Liquidation of the company/cessation of the business
- Active intervention of the chargees (eg appointing a receiver)
- If the charge provides, at the time when the provision states
- A different charge crystallises, leading to liquidation/cessation

Principal disadvantages of a floating charge

- [X] Until crystallisation, assets making up the security are uncertain
- [X] Chargeholder is less important than other creditors
- [X] May become invalid if liquidation arises within 12 months (this period is only six months with a fixed charge.)

Unsecured debentureholders rights

- Sue the company/seize property
- Petition for compulsory liquidation
- Apply for administration order as a temporary reprieve to rescue the company

Secured debentureholders rights

- Seize legally charged asset
- Sell that asset (if there is a deed)
- Appoint a receiver of the asset (provided there is no administrator)
- Appoint an administrator (floating chargeholders)

17: Capital maintenance and dividend law

Topic List

Reduction of share capital

Dividends

Reduction of share capital and dividend law are probably the most complicated areas of the syllabus, but there are some straightforward rules which you can apply. Remember that in most issues relating to capital maintenance, the rules are designed for the protection of creditors and members.

Capital maintenance: Companies should not make payments out of capital because this threatens creditors.
Basic principle on capital maintenance: Limited companies should not be allowed to make payments out of capital.
Exception to basic principle: Reducing share capital (not restricted in articles, special resolution, court approval).

Method	What happens	Effects
Extinguish or reduce liability on partly paid shares.	Eg Company has nominal value £1 shares 75p paid up. Either (a) reduce nominal value to 75p; or (b) reduce nominal value to figure between 75p and £1.	Company gives up claim for amount not paid up (no return to shareholders).
Pay off part of paid-up share capital out of surplus assets.	Eg Company reduces nominal value of fully paid shares from £1 to 70p and repays this amount to shareholders.	Assets of company are reduced (by 30p in £).
Cancel paid-up share capital which has been lost or no longer represented by available assets.	Eg Company has £1 nominal fully paid shares but net assets only worth 50p per share. Difference = debit balance on reserves. Company reduces nominal value to 50p, and applies amount to write off debit balance.	Company can resume payments out of future profits without having to make good past losses.

The reduction must be approved by the **court,** whom must protect the interests of creditors. Private companies may avoid going to court by issuing a **solvency statement**.

Dividends, profits and reserves

Dividends represent a debt of the company once they are declared and due for payment.

A **dividend** is an amount payable to shareholders from profits or other distributable reserves.

Distributable reserves are accumulated realised profits less accumulated realised losses.

Undistributable reserves are: share premium account, capital redemption reserve, revaluation reserve, and any other reserve made undistributable by law or the company's constitution.

Notes

18: Company directors

Directors run the company as its agents. They are officers of the company and may be executive or non-executives. Normally one director acts as Managing Director.

The powers of directors can seem a difficult area. Remember the following three key things:

Topic List

The role of directors

Appointment of directors

Vacation of office

Powers of directors

Duties of directors

- **Directors' powers** are usually **set** by the **articles**
- **Members have some control** through their appointment/removal **of directors** and by changing the articles
- Directors are **agents** of the company. Third parties have **protection** when dealing with them

*Directors have **duties** as agents of the company. They also have duties under various statutory provisions.*

Director

A person who is responsible for the overall direction of the company's affairs. All companies must have at least one. Public companies need two. A director is an officer of the company. At least one director must be a natural person.

De jure director

A person who is expressly appointed by the company as a director.

De facto director

A person who is held out by a company to be a director and who performs the functions of a director although they have not been validly appointed as such.

Shadow director

A person whose instructions the other directors are accustomed to follow. This rule is in place to prevent a person from not taking up appointment as a director, but using their position (say as major shareholder) to manipulate the board of directors.

De facto/non-executive/shadow directors still owe statutory and fiduciary directors' duties.

Executive director

Executive directors perform specific roles in a company under service contracts requiring regular involvement in management.

Non-executive director

A non-executive director does not usually have a management function other than attending board meetings.

Board of Directors

The elected representative of the shareholders acting collectively in the management of a company's affairs.

Chief Executive Officer/Managing Director

One of the directors of the company appointed to carry out overall day to day management functions. The CEO/MD has wider apparent authority than other directors.

Methods of appointment

A company's first directors are appointed as part of its formation via the **statement of proposed officers.**

Thereafter, appointment of directors is as the articles provide (election of directors in general meeting, or co-option by directors).

Rotation

Model articles provide for rotation of directors of PLCs:

- At the first AGM, all the directors shall retire
- Any directors appointed by the other directors since the last AGM shall retire
- Directors who were not appointed or re-elected at one of the two preceding AGMs shall retire

All directors selected for retirement by rotation can still offer themselves for re-election.

Publicity

Companies must give 14 days' notice to the Registrar of changes in directors.

The directors must keep the register of directors and secretary (which can be inspected by any member of the public) at the registered office.

Remuneration of directors

- Fees
- Reasonable expenses
- Usually have written service contracts – open to members' inspection. May receive contractual or non-contractual (approved by members) compensation for loss of office.
- Directors' remuneration report published in annual report to members of quoted companies

Vacation of office

- Resignation
- Not offering to be re-elected
- Death
- Dissolution of the company
- **Disqualification**
- **Removal from office**

A director may be removed from office by an **ordinary resolution (special notice)**.

Grounds under articles

The articles may provide that a director is disqualified if they become bankrupt, resign in writing, or at the resolve of other directors if they are absent from board meetings for three months.

Disqualification may also be under **statute**.

This important member power given by s168 CA 2006 is restricted by three limitations:

- To propose a removal resolution, the members must call a meeting and so must hold 10% of the paid up share capital or voting rights.
- Once a meeting has been convened, 100 members with an average of £100 share capital may request the resolution (this is true of any resolution not just the removal of a director).
- If the director is a member, they may have weighted voting rights to prevent removal.
- A member director may also be protected by class rights attaching to their shares.

Disqualification of directors under statute

Under CDDA 1986 the court **may** make an order for disqualification.

Potential grounds for disqualification

- Person convicted of an indictable offence connected with a company
- Person in persistent default in relation to the provisions of company law
- Person has been guilty of fraudulent trading
- After investigation, the Secretary of State believes it to be in the public interest
- Director has been involved in competition violations
- Director of an insolvent company has participated in wrongful trading

Compulsory grounds for disqualification

The court **must** make an order where a person has been a director of a company which has become insolvent, or where their conduct makes them unfit to be a director. The **length of disqualification period** is generally at the discretion of the court (minimum disqualification: two years).

Mitigating factors:

Lack of dishonesty, loss of own money in the transaction, absence of personal gain, efforts to mitigate the situation, likelihood of re-offending, proceedings taking a long time.

Examples

Directors have been disqualified for: insider dealing, failing to keep proper accounting records, failing to read the accounts, irregularities connected with lending the company's money.

The directors' powers are defined by the **articles of association**.

↓

Model articles state that the directors are usually authorised to:

'Manage the business of the company'

and

'Exercise all the powers of the company for any purpose connected with the company's business'.

Statutory restrictions on directors' powers

Many transactions (eg altering the articles) can only be effected by a decision of the company in general meeting, often via a special resolution (75% majority).

Members' control of directors

Members have control over the board of directors by retaining the power to remove directors under s168, and by having the power to change the articles by special resolution. Directors can also be members, but they don't have to be.

Restriction on directors' powers in the articles

The articles can contain restrictions, eg, a maximum amount that the directors can borrow without the consent of the members in general meeting.

Directors must exercise their powers:

- In the interests of the company
- For a proper purpose (the purpose for which the power was given)

CEO/MD's powers

The CEO/MD is an **agent** of the company. Therefore these rules apply:

Actual authority ➤ What the board has given them

Apparent authority ➤ To make business contracts for the company. (No other director has this general apparent authority)

Holding out

Under the rules of apparent authority, if the board allows a director to hold themselves out as being a CEO/MD and takes no steps to correct that impression, that director will have the authority of a CEO/MD outlined above.

Other working directors

Only have the specific apparent authority as agents which attaches to their management position.

Case box

Freeman & Lockyer v Buckhurst Park Properties (Mangal) Ltd 1964

Conditions to claim holding out

1. Representation was made to the claimant that the director had authority to make such a contract

2. The person who made the representation had actual authority to manage the business

3. Claimant was induced by the representation

4. The constitution would not restrict the board giving such authority

Fiduciary duty

A duty imposed upon certain persons because of the **position of trust and confidence** in which they stand in relation to each other. Directors are said to hold a fiduciary position because they act as agents of the company.

Statutory duties of directors

Under the Companies Act 2006 directors have seven statutory duties to the company:

- Act within powers (s171)
- Promote the success of the company (s172)
- Exercise independent judgement (s173)
- Exercise reasonable skill, care and diligence (s174)
- Avoid conflicts of interest (s175)
- Not to accept benefits from third parties (s176)
- Declare an interest in a proposed transaction or arrangement (s177)

Remedies for breach of duty

Action may be taken by shareholders.

Director may have to:

- Account to company for personal gain
- Indemnify the company

Company might be able to:

- Rescind the contract
- Have the courts declare it *ultra vires* and therefore unlawful

Where directors have breached a duty, the **company may authorise or ratify the act**.

This can be done by:

- Provision in the **articles**
- Passing a **resolution**

This right is **restricted if the directors, who are also members**, defraud the company and then ratify their acts in general meeting. It may also be restricted if the directors' acts altered the share balance to allow subsequent ratification.

Duty of care (s174)

Directors should show the objective degree of skill as could reasonably be expected from a competent person in that role, or a higher personal degree of skill if the director has particular expertise.

Directors' personal liability for company debts

May arise from:

- Lifting the veil
- A provision in the constitution
- A special resolution
- Some insolvency situations

Notes

19: Other company officers

Topic List

Company secretary

Company auditor

You may face questions on company secretaries and auditors in your exam. In both cases you should learn about their appointment and duties. The removal of an auditor is also important.

Company Secretary

Every public company must have a company secretary with requisite skill and knowledge. Private companies are not required to have a company secretary.

Responsibility for:

- Statutory registers and returns
- Organising board and general meetings

Company secretaries have ostensible authority to enter the company into contracts connected with the administration of the company:

Panorama Developments (Guildford) Ltd v Fidelis Furnishing Fabrics Ltd 1971

Qualification

- Employment as a plc's secretary for three/five years preceding appointment
- Membership of one of a list of qualifying bodies, such as the ACCA
- Qualification as a solicitor or barrister in the UK
- Employment in a position, or membership of a professional body that, in the opinion of the directors, appears to qualify that person to act as company secretary

A sole director of a private company cannot also be the company secretary, but a company can have two or more joint secretaries. A corporation can fulfil the role of company secretary.

Auditor

A person independent of the company. They are not permitted to be a company officer by law and by the rules of their recognised supervisory body.

Appointment

Every company which is not exempt must have an auditor.

Appointment is made by:

- **Shareholders** (normally)
- **Directors**
- **Secretary of State**

Termination of office

Removal by ordinary resolution with special notice. Auditor's rights:

- Submit a statement of circumstances surrounding their removal
- Written statement to members
- Speak at general meeting

Resignation in writing to registered office

- Circulate a written statement to members
- Requisition a general meeting
- Speak at general meeting

Not seeking re-election

A written statement of circumstances is always required when auditors leave.

The auditor has the **right** to obtain explanations from officers of the company and the **duty** to report on the truth and fairness of the accounts.

19: Other company officers

Notes

20: Company meetings and resolutions

Topic List

Types of meeting

Types of resolution

Convening/quorum/proxies/
procedures

*The legal details regarding meetings can seem confusing.
Therefore, focus on the key issues which you must know:*

- *The distinction between types of meeting*
- *The types of resolution that can be passed*

The importance of meetings

The company is managed by **directors**.

However, decisions which affect the existence, structure and scope of the company are reserved to the **members** in **general meeting**.

Members can, to an extent, exercise control over directors in general meeting. They can:

- **Remove** them (ordinary resolution)
- **Approve** their behaviour, eg to
  - Exceed their power given in the articles
  - Allot shares
  - Make contracts where they have a personal interest
  - Grant a long term service agreement

Annual general meeting (AGM)

Statutorily protected general meeting held annually by public companies, called by the directors.

General meeting

General meetings which can be called in response to a need arising by either a members' requisition or by the directors.

Members holding 5% of the voting rights or of at least 100 in number with an average of £100 paid up capital may requisition a resolution to be considered at an AGM or general meeting, at least six weeks in advance.

Members may circulate a statement of <1,000 words to accompany the notice.

Ordinary (all companies)	Requires simple (50%+) majority of votes cast 14 days' notice
Special (all companies)	Requires 75% majority of votes cast 14 days' notice
Written (private companies)	Used for all resolutions (ordinary and special) except those needing special notice (director's and auditor's removal)

The texts of **special** resolutions must be **set out in full** in the **notice** convening the meeting.

All special resolutions must be delivered to the Registrar for filing. It is rare that ordinary resolutions are filed.

When **special notice** is required for an ordinary resolution (eg for a member to remove a director/auditor) the member must give the company 28 days notice, and the company must give all members 21 days' notice.

Requires a 50% majority for ordinary business and a 75% majority for special business

Members holding 5% of the voting rights may request a written resolution and circulate a statement of <1,000 words to accompany the notice which must be sent to all members within 21 days.

Rules concerning calling a meeting

AGM (public companies only)

Timing
- Must be held each year
- Within six months of year-end

Notice
- In writing or as articles prescribe
- At least 21 days' notice
- Notice must specify it is an AGM

Business
- Declaration of dividends
- Election of directors
- Appointment of auditors

General meetings

The directors may call a general meeting whenever they see fit, giving 14 clear days' notice.

The following rules apply for **members** requisitioning a general meeting.

Shareholding of requisitioners
- Must represent 5% of the paid up share capital or voting rights

Requisition by members
- Must provide a statement of the general business to be conducted
- Must provide a text of the proposed resolution

Date of requisitioned meeting
- Notice for a meeting must be sent within 21 days of requisition
- Meeting within 28 days of notice

Convening

- Called by a competent person
- Clear notice given to members
- Notice must be sent to all entitled to receive it
- Notice must contain certain facts
- Notice may be sent electronically (email and website)

Proxies

- Any member can appoint a proxy
- The proxy does not have to be a member
- Proxy may vote, speak and demand a poll

Quorum

- One person cannot generally be a meeting
- An exception to this is for single member private companies
- The articles usually fix a quorum for meetings

Procedures

- Chairman must preside
- Show of hands vote means all present get one vote
- Poll vote means votes are weighted in relation to shareholding
- Minutes must be kept
- The assent principle allows a unanimous decision to stand

Notes

21: Insolvency and administration

Topic List

Liquidation

Compulsory liquidation

Voluntary liquidation

Compulsory & voluntary liquidation

Administration

Once you have understood that there are two main types of liquidation (compulsory and voluntary) and two types of voluntary liquidation (members' and creditors') it should be straightforward to learn the features of each of them.

Company administration is also important in this syllabus.

Liquidation

A company is dissolved and its affairs wound up (hence it is sometimes referred to as winding up). The assets are realised, debts are paid from the proceeds and any surplus amounts are paid to members.

There are two main types of liquidation (compulsory and voluntary). When a company is liquidated, a **liquidator** must be appointed.

A liquidator must be an authorised insolvency practitioner. They have a **statutory duty** to report directors of an **insolvent company** if they are considered unfit to be involved in management.

BUT

A company does not have to be insolvent to be liquidated.

Once a company enters liquidation:

- No share dealings
- Communications must state the company is in liquidation
- Director's power to manage ceases

Compulsory liquidation

Various parties may apply to the court for a company to be wound up. Key reasons:

- Company is **unable to pay its debts** (creditors)
- It is **just and equitable** to wind up the company (members)
- A public limited company has traded without a **trading certificate** > one year
- It is in the **public interest** to wind up the company

Company cannot pay debts

A creditor can show a company is unable to pay its debts in three situations:

- A written demand is served for £750 at the registered office and the debt is still unpaid within 21 days
- There are no assets against which to enforce payment
- The creditor proves to the court that the company is unable to pay its debts.

When the court approves the order:

- Official receiver is the liquidator
- Liquidation from date petition presented
- Subsequent sale of assets void
- Legal proceedings halted
- Employees dismissed
- Floating charges crystallise

The liquidation is deemed to have started when the order was first applied for. The official receiver holds **meetings** with the creditors and contributories (members) who can appoint their own liquidator. Creditors' choice takes priority. The official receiver **must investigate the affairs** of the company and may report to the court, seeking a public examination of those responsible. They may apply to the Registrar for early dissolution if assets do not cover their expenses.

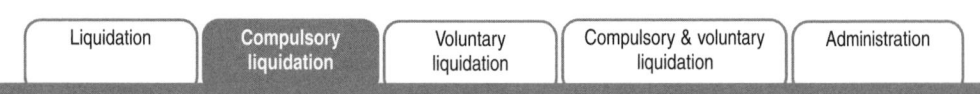

Just and equitable compulsory liquidation

A member who is dissatisfied with the directors/controlling shareholders can petition for a just and equitable winding up of the company.

The petitioner must show that **no other remedy is acceptable**. Winding up an otherwise healthy company is a big step, so incidences of this are rare.

Case box

Re German Date Coffee Co 1882

Re Yenidje Tobacco Co Ltd 1916

Ebrahimi v Westbourne Galleries Ltd 1973

Examples of orders made

- Main purpose of company has gone
- Company formed for illegal purposes
- Complete management deadlock
- Understandings between members/directors unfairly breached by lawful action

Order of payments on liquidation

1 Costs of liquidation

2 Preferential debts (employee pay)

3 Floating charges (subject to prescribed part)

4 Unsecured creditors

5 Deferred debts (dividends and interest)

6 Distribution to members

Members' voluntary liquidation

The company is solvent but the members decide to liquidate anyway.

Mostly commonly achieved by passing a **special resolution** (75%).

Directors must issue a **declaration of solvency** that debts can be paid up in full in a period < 12 months.

Creditors play no part in a members' winding up, as it is assumed the debts will be paid in full.

Creditors' voluntary liquidation

The company is insolvent and the members agree to wind it up.

Special resolution passed (75%).

Meeting of creditors convened to resolve to wind up, appoint a liquidator and nominate five representatives to form a liquidation committee.

If the creditors do not appoint a liquidator, the members should.

Making a declaration of solvency without reasonable grounds is a criminal offence.

21: Insolvency and administration

Control	Compulsory liquidations are controlled by the court, members' voluntary liquidations are controlled by the members and creditors control a creditors' voluntary winding up.
Timing	A voluntary winding up commences on the day the resolution to wind up is passed. It is not retrospective. A compulsory winding up commences on the day the petition was presented to the court.
Liquidator	The official receiver plays no role in a voluntary winding up. The members or creditors select the liquidator who is not an court officer.
Legal proceedings	There is no automatic stay of legal proceedings against the company nor are previous dispositions or seizure of its assets void in a voluntary winding up. However the liquidator has a general right to apply to the court to make any order which the court can make in a compulsory liquidation.
Management and staff	In any liquidation the liquidator replaces the directors in the management of the company (unless they decide to retain them). The employees are not automatically dismissed by the commencement of voluntary liquidation. However, insolvent liquidation may amount to repudiation of their contracts of employment (and provisions of the statutory employment protection code apply).

Administration puts an insolvency practitioner in control of the company with a defined programme for rescuing it from insolvency, as a going concern (it cannot already be in liquidation). The administrator will seek to save the company, **or** to achieve a better result for creditors than immediate liquidation, **or** to realise property for distribution to creditors.

Effect of administration	Advantages of an administration
■ A moratorium commences (no creditors may enforce debts against the company)	☑ The company is not dissolved
■ Items with charges may be sold (fixed chargeholders to give permission)	☑ It provides breathing space to attempt a rescue of the company
■ The powers of management are subjugated to the appointed administrator, who must act in the interests of all creditors	☑ Past transactions of the company can be challenged
	☑ It allows creditors to continue to trade with the company if the rescue is successful
■ Outstanding petitions for the winding up of the company are dismissed	☑ Members continue to own shares in the company which may be successful in the future

The court may be petitioned for an administration order by:

- The company (a 50% majority of members)
- The directors
- Creditors
- The Magistrates' Court (for non-payment of fines) NOT by individual members.

Appointment of administrators without reference to the court

Certain parties can appoint an administrator without going to court.

Floating chargeholders

May appoint an administrator if:

- They have given two days' notice to holders of prior floating charges (unless they consent)
- The floating charge is enforceable

After two days' notice, an appointing floating chargeholder must file certain documents at the court making the appointment valid.

Company/directors

May (depending on articles) appoint if:

- No administration/moratorium in last 12 months
- Company cannot pay debts
- No petitions for winding up/administration have been made
- No liquidator/administrative receiver/administrator already in office

The company/directors must give floating chargeholders notice so that they may block appointment if they wish. They then file the appropriate documents with the court to make the appointment valid.

Administrator's duties

As soon as reasonably practicable after their appointment, they must send notice of it to:

- The company
- Each creditor
- The Registrar (within seven days)

They must also **publish** news of the appointment.

They must ensure all company documents publicise that it is '**in administration**'.

They must consider the **statements of affairs** submitted to them and set out proposals to achieve the aims of administration.

Administrator's proposals

- Must set out proposals to achieve the aim of administration OR why they do not consider it reasonable or practical that the company be rescued

- Must not affect the right of a secured creditor to enforce their security, or result in preferential debt losing priority to non-preferential debt, or to one preferential debt being paid proportionately less than another

- Must be provided if requested by the administrator. It is in a prescribed form and contains details of company property, debts and liabilities, company creditors and security given for debts.

Administrator's powers

To do anything necessarily expedient for the management of the affairs, business and property of the company:

- Remove/appoint directors
- Call meeting of creditors/members
- Apply to the court for direction
- Make payments to secured/preferential creditors
- Make payments to unsecured creditors (with court permission)

End of administration

When:

- Administration has been successful
- 12 months have passed since appointment
- The administrator or a creditor applies to court to end the appointment
- An improper motive of the applicant for applying for administration is discovered

Interaction with other insolvency procedures

- Prevents voluntary winding up application and order for compulsory winding up
- Prevents appointment of administrative receivers

The administrator must call a meeting of creditors within ten weeks of appointment to approve the proposals.

22: Fraudulent and criminal behaviour

Topic List

Insider dealing

Market abuse

Money laundering

Bribery

Criminal activity relating to companies

Crime, as we know, is conduct prohibited by the law. Here we shall look at five aspects of financial crime; insider dealing, market abuse, money laundering, bribery and criminal activity relating to companies.

Insider dealing

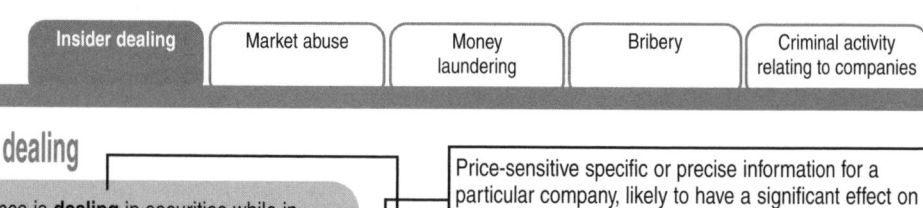

The offence is **dealing** in securities while in possession of **inside information** as an **insider**, the securities being price-affected by the information.

Price-sensitive specific or precise information for a particular company, likely to have a significant effect on price if made public.

Director, employee, shareholder; or obtained through employment, office or profession; or obtained from one of the above.

In the UK the rules on insider dealing are contained in the Criminal Justice Act 1993.

'**Dealing**' in this context includes encouraging someone else to purchase the shares whether on behalf of the insider or not, with the reasonable belief that the person would deal.

Defences include not expecting a profit to be made, having reasonable belief that the information was public, acting despite the information.

Problems with the law

- Determining whether information is precise enough to have been inside information
- 'Price-sensitive issue' limits the scope of the law to fundamental matters such as takeovers
- The offence of 'market abuse' was introduced into the UK to deal with these deficiencies

Market abuse

Behaviour that satisfies one or more prescribed conditions that are regarded as a failure on the part of the person concerned to observe the standard of behaviour reasonably expected of a person in their position in relation to the market.

Examples

- Misuse of information
- Market distortion
- Manipulating transactions
- Recklessly manipulating devices
- Dissemination of information

22: Fraudulent and criminal behaviour

The rules on **money laundering** in the UK are found mainly in the Proceeds of Crime Act 2002, the Criminal Justice Act 1993 and the Money Laundering Regulations 2007. New legislation is being introduced in response to International and European measures.

> Accountants and other professionals have a duty to report money laundering. Failure in relation to that duty is a criminal offence which may result in a prison term of up to five years.

Money laundering

The term given to attempts to make the proceeds of crime appear respectable. There are five UK offences:

- **Acquisition**, **possession** or use of such proceeds
- **Assisting** another to retain such proceeds
- **Concealing** such proceeds
- **Failure to report** knowledge/suspicion of ML
- **Tipping off** (warning a suspected launderer)

There are three phases in the process of money laundering:

- **Placement** – The actual disposal of the proceeds of initial illegal activity
- **Layering** – The transfer of monies to conceal the original source
- **Integration** – Having been layered, the money has the appearance of legitimate funds

Laundering ←

Companies need to take action to be aware of anti-money laundering regulations.

Bribery

The **Bribery Act 2010** created four offences concerning bribery.

Bribing another person

Offering financial or other advantages to induce another to perform a relevant function or activity improperly.

Being bribed

Requesting or accepting financial or other advantages in return for performing a relevant function or activity improperly.

Bribing a foreign public official

Offering financial or other advantages to a foreign official with the intention of influencing that person in their official capacity. A foreign public official is anyone holding a legislative, administrative or judicial position.

Corporate failure to prevent bribery

This is a corporate offence which is commited by an organisation that fails to prevent a bribery offence being commited by anyone that represents the organisation. An organisation has a defence if it has 'adequate procedures' in place to prevent bribery.

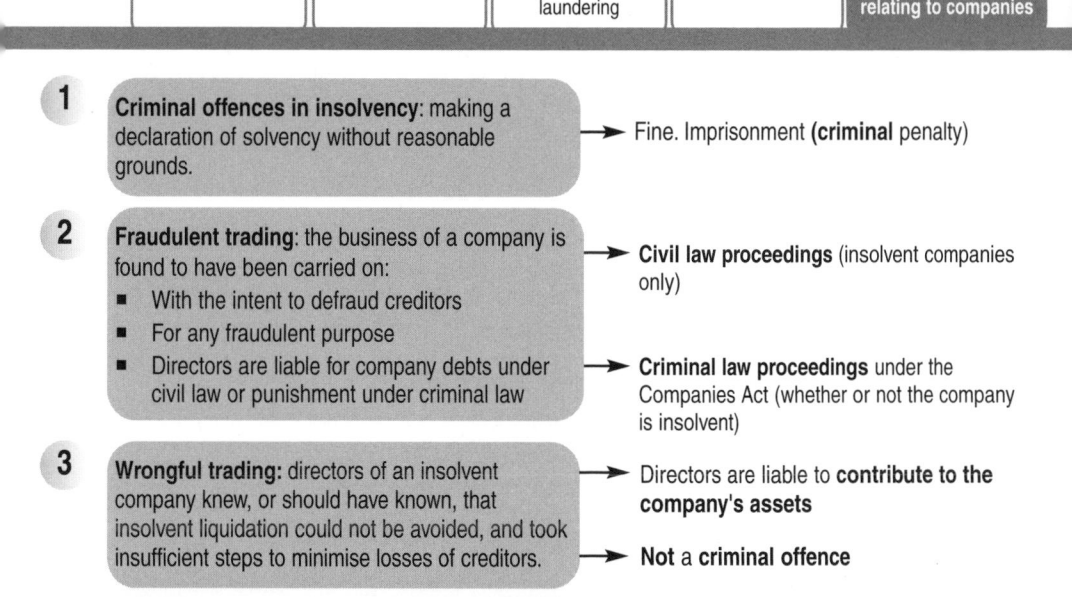

1 **Criminal offences in insolvency**: making a declaration of solvency without reasonable grounds.

→ Fine. Imprisonment **(criminal** penalty)

2 **Fraudulent trading**: the business of a company is found to have been carried on:
- With the intent to defraud creditors
- For any fraudulent purpose
- Directors are liable for company debts under civil law or punishment under criminal law

→ **Civil law proceedings** (insolvent companies only)

→ **Criminal law proceedings** under the Companies Act (whether or not the company is insolvent)

3 **Wrongful trading**: directors of an insolvent company knew, or should have known, that insolvent liquidation could not be avoided, and took insufficient steps to minimise losses of creditors.

→ Directors are liable to **contribute to the company's assets**

→ **Not** a **criminal offence**

Other offences in relation to winding up

- Managing whilst disqualified
- Phoenix companies
- Fraud and deception
- Defrauding creditors
- Misconduct during a liquidation
- Falsification of company books
- Omissions

Where there is evidence that a company or partnership has committed certain offences, such as fraud, money laundering, bribery or forgery, it is possible for the prosecution and the organisation to make a **deferred prosecution agreement** (DPA) under the **Crime and Courts Act 2013**.

Such agreements mean that the **organisation admits wrongdoing** but stops short of pleading guilty to the offence. In return, a Judge awards a fine against the business but **no criminal prosecution takes place**.

Companies Act offences

The Companies Act 2006 created a number of offences in relation to the management of a company.

- Failure to keep adequate **company records** or their falsification
- Failure to keep adequate **accounting records**
- Failure to make required **trading disclosures**
- Failure to **file accounts** on time
- Making **false disclosures** in company reports
- Failure to deliver the **annual return** on time

Notes

Notes

Notes

Notes

Notes

Notes

Notes

Notes